1001 WAYS
TO GET MORE CUSTOMERS

1001 Proven, Practical Tips to
Generate Customers for Your Business

JONATHAN JAY

NABO

Copyright © 2014 NABO (UK) Ltd.

First published in Great Britain in 2014
Jonathan Jay
NABO (UK) Ltd
12 Blades Court
121 Deodar Road
Putney
London
SW15 2NU
info@nabo.biz
www.nabo.biz

Designed by NABO.

Printed and bound in Great Britain by
CPI Group (UK) Ltd, Croydon, CR0 4YY

British Library Cataloguing in Publication Data.
ISBN 978-0-9566192-4-2

Contents

To apply for a free implementation session **worth £495** where we show you how everything in this book can be done for you, go to **completedigitalmarketingsystem.com/121**

3

Introduction

As a business owner, your quest for entrepreneurial success ultimately boils down to just one thing: your ability to get customers. If you could get all the customers you need flowing into your business 24/7, it would solve your financial challenges forever. You and those you care about will have achieved the ultimate entrepreneurial goal: total financial freedom!

'1001 Ways to Get Customers' is your step by step guide to achieving that freedom. Most business owners only use one or two methods to attract customers. You're about to access hundreds of possible ways to use online marketing to bring the customers you need streaming into your business. From transforming your website to mastering Google, understanding the power of online video and duplicating the email and social media strategies of the most successful entrepreneurs, this is your comprehensive guide to running a stunningly successful business.

While many business owners struggle, the top 1% get to choose how many customers they have. As a result they get to choose how much money is in their bank account – and how often and how hard they work. The entrepreneur dream can be yours – once you crack the customer code. This is the book that gives you the code and unlocks the door to your own personal customer goldmine.

To apply for a free implementation session **worth £495** where we show you how everything in this book can be done for you, go to **completedigitalmarketingsystem.com/121**

5

Chapter 1

Marketing

In a Nutshell

Marketing is a lot less complicated than you may have been led to believe.

Essentially, marketing is:

- Identifying your target market (those people who want your product or service, that you can reach easily, and who can afford your product/service)

- Discovering the needs and/or wants of your target audience

- Developing and then executing a plan to create a relevant and unique offering

- Creating and retaining loyal customers who actively engage with your brand

In other words, marketing is about creating a positive relationship with your target audience.

Most importantly, marketing is essential for your business. Without it, your business is going to struggle to stay afloat. Use the following tips to grow your business and increase your profits.

To apply for a free implementation session **worth £495** where we show you how everything in this book can be done for you, go to **completedigitalmarketingsystem.com/121**

7

1. Understand the buying cycle

The buying cycle is the process prospects go through when they realise they've got a problem that needs fixing or a want that must be satisfied. It has five stages:

- Recognising there's a problem/want

- Searching for solutions to the problem/want

- Creating a shortlist of solutions then picking one

- Finding vendors who provide the chosen solution. Selecting one vendor

- Making a purchase/hiring the service provider

2. Don't create a product or service that suits you

If you want to make money, you need to sell your product or service to other people. What they like, want or need is more important than what you want, like, or need. Design everything to suit your prospective customers, not yourself, your employees or your family/friends.

3. You can't sell to everyone

Your product or service will only ever appeal to a subsection of any population. For that reason, it's a huge mistake to try and appeal to an entire population. To be successful, you should focus on the subsection and forget the rest.

4. Concentrate on your target market

Your target market consists of your ideal customers – those people who are looking for a product or service like yours to solve their problem.

5. You can have more than one target market

Sometimes you have more than one target market. Many companies create a primary and secondary target market. The primary target market receives most of the focus and budget. However, these businesses recognise that there are other targets that require some attention if they are to be successful.

6. Make sure you can deliver what your target market wants

You must be able to deliver the product and service your target market really wants. If there is a disconnect between what your target wants and what you can deliver, your marketing plan and ultimately, your business, will fail.

7. If you provide a service, understand how your prospective buyers choose providers

It's crucial to understand how your potential buyers identify and learn about the service providers they hire. You need to know this information so that you don't waste time, money, and energy on marketing methods that won't have any impact on your prospects' buying decisions. Generally, the seven most common ways decision-makers identify and learn about professional service providers are:

- Referrals from colleagues and others in their network

- Previous experience

- Research within their own organisation

- Advice from industry analysts

- Online research

- Business articles and trade reports

- Trade shows, exhibitions and conferences

8. Know what factors influence clients' hiring decisions

Clients typically base their actual hiring decisions on the following:

- A professional service provider's experience in the client's industry or business

- Overall cost or fees

To apply for a free implementation session **worth £495** where we show you how everything in this book can be done for you, go to **completedigitalmarketingsystem.com/121**

9

- Experience in the specific area where the client needs help

- Overall value the professional service provider can deliver

- The variety of services offered by the professional service provider

- Written proposal

- Proximity of the service provider to the client's premises

- The quality of the service provider's website

9. Identify your niche market

No matter what you sell – even if it's a service that everybody can use – you will be much more successful if you learn niche marketing. It is a multi-part process that includes locating unique markets with untapped profit potential, learning everything about them, and making irresistible offers to them.

The trick to niche marketing is that the message is specific and highly targeted. It's extremely personal as in *"I'm talking to YOU"* personal and your content 'speaks' to the unique needs of your target. That's what makes it compelling.

10. Sell in more than one niche

If you have the infrastructure to support multiple niches you can sell into many niches, but you must give each niche the feeling that this is all you do and that you do it "especially for them."

When looking at markets to go after, you must make sure that there are ways to find out who the prospects are in that niche and whether the niche is profitable.

11. Don't make your marketing message too general

If you get off-track and allow your marketing to become fuzzy or too general it becomes more and more difficult for prospects and clients to distinguish your service offering from any other. Prospects want to believe that somebody can truly fill their needs. If they believe you understand them, you serve their needs. Equally, if you've served somebody just like them, they will be more likely to try your business than the one that does not meet their specific needs.

12. Find under-served niches

To succeed in a big way, you need to find an underserved niche and provide information that is desperately wanted and needed.

13. Steer clear of being a generalist in any market

If you're suffering from a knee injury, you're more likely to look for a medical practitioner who specialises in treating that kind of injury than you are to turn to your local GP for help. The same principle applies to your prospective clients. They want someone who can solve their specific problem. The danger with being a generalist is that while it might give you a bigger market to aim your service at, it also brings with it greater competition. Rather than being a generalist, become a specialist in one sector of the market and then when you've built up a client base there, consider adding another sector.

14. Narrowing your focus brings more success

When you identify a niche, you can become known in that niche, and then clients will begin to call you. Contrary to popular opinion, narrowing your focus will actually result in more not less clients. A good niche will give you between three and 10 times more clients than general or unfocused marketing. A good niche will provide you with a long-term, sustainable advantage in your marketing that will position you apart from all the competition and attract an endless stream of prospects.

15. Know how to pick the most profitable niche

The key elements for a profitable niche are:

- Size – the niche must be big enough to supply you with as many clients as you need.

To apply for a free implementation session **worth £495** where we show you how everything in this book can be done for you, go to **completedigitalmarketingsystem.com/121**

11

- Money – the people in your niche must be able to afford your fees or prices. For example, 'marketing consultant for IT businesses in a specific region' has a vastly greater potential for income than 'marketing consultant for start-up companies' (because start-up companies tend to have shoe-string budgets).

- Reach – you must be able to reach your clients easily through targeted promotions. For instance, you can offer your services to an international audience via the internet so long as you have the ability to reach your prospects wherever they are in the world.

- Contactable – you must be able to contact your clients by telephone, the internet, or face to face.

- Burning need – is there an intense, perceived need for the niche in the minds of your prospects? Are they truly concerned with the issue you can help them solve with your service? The more intense their pain or, conversely, the more attractive the benefit you help them realise, the more quickly the niche will respond to your efforts.

- Under-served – how many similar services are already being offered to the niche? Your business will grow faster in an under-served industry than in a highly developed one that has many providers trying to meet the given need.

- Precedent – are there already successful businesses operating in this niche? If so, it suggests that people will pay to have a specific need addressed.

- Be the first – take a successful niche and narrow it further.

- Narrow focus – it's much better to offer your service to a narrow professional industry (divorce lawyers) than to a broad group (all lawyers).

- Industry focus – are members of your niche from a single professional group or industry? If you focus on a subset of a specific professional group, the niche is much easier to penetrate. You can email a specific newsletter to your target group. You can market the niche through its local, national, and even international professional organisations. You can forge alliances with suppliers who serve the same niche.

- A coherent group – it's a major advantage if members of your proposed niche feel they belong to a coherent group. Members are more likely to forward your promotional material to others if they know who the others are.

- Improved financial or performance benefits – can you help your niche to make money or improve performance? While they're not essential criterion for being hired, it's easier for clients to justify hiring you month after month if you're helping them to make more money or perform better professionally.

16. Always research a niche before launching your business

Research your niche. Interview at least three prospects to identify what their needs are, how best to communicate with the niche, learn more about the competition, how to quickly position yourself as an expert within the niche, and how best to package your service as the solution to the niche's greatest unmet, tangible needs that they are prepared to pay to resolve.

Test your solution. Conduct a mini service launch to test the interest in the market and to obtain testimonials.

17. Get known in your niche

Seek every opportunity to speak, write, or share your knowledge with your target audience to increase your exposure and solidify your position as an expert solution provider to this niche. The greater the 'expert' profile you have with the group, the more responsive they will be to your invitation to do business with you.

18. Understand your market

Once you've narrowed down who you want to sell a particular product to, you should identify that market's wants. When you begin marketing to the most important wants and considerations your market has, you automatically become more effective, more efficient, and more profitable (and get more recognition as the expert!). You'll waste less time and get much more mileage for your marketing time and effort.

19. Create a profile of your ideal client

Compile a very detailed profile of the Ideal Client for your business. List both external factors (demographics) and internal factors (psychographics).

- What are all the issues, problems and challenges your prospects face? What keeps them up at night?

- What do they want? What do they need?

- What is the main outcome your prospects might want as a result of using your service?

- What benefits do they want to get from using a service like yours?

- What is your prospect's main concern? (Price, delivery, performance, reliability, service maintenance, quality, efficiency?)

- What motivates your prospective buyer?

20. Know your competition

This is one of the most critical and yet most overlooked steps in marketing a business effectively. Many business owners don't have any idea who their real competition is, how long they've been in business, what they have to offer the marketplace, or the advantages or disadvantages of doing business with them.

Similarly, too many business owners think they know their competition but don't research them often enough. This means they miss opportunities to fill gaps in the market left by their competitors. What's more, when prospective or existing clients want to know what their company does better than the competition, they are at a disadvantage because they don't know.

It's imperative that you constantly update the information you have about your top competitors. Gather as much objective and useful information as you can about your competition.

Make sure you can answer the following questions:

- What's their product or service? (Are they in direct competition with you? Does their product or service address a problem in the same way your service does?)

- What is their revenue?

- How have they grown or shrunk over the past 12 months, and over the past five years?

- What is their market share? (This is often more relevant than their revenue. Some industries are tracked by analysts, which makes the information easier to find.)

- What do their clients think about them? How do they treat their clients? What do they do to keep their clients' loyalty?

- Is your client service better than the competition? Do you give more value added service? Do you offer volume discount pricing? Do you have a longer-term relationship with your clients?

- Does your company make it easier in any way for a client to do business in any of the following areas: additional education, free consultations, bonuses, incentives, better sales terms, longer hours, better client service and after-sales service, returns policy, or a rewards club?

21. Become a prospective buyer for your competition

Contact your competition to determine how good (or bad) they are at establishing relationships with prospects.

- Do they try to get you to come to their office, shop, or set up an appointment for a salesperson to meet you?

- Do they ask when the service you're using will expire or need renewing?

- Do they question you about your immediate and long-term needs and wants?

- Do they only provide quotes for the service you enquire about?

- Do they give you reasons for doing business with them rather than other companies?

- Do they attempt to capture your name, address, phone number, and email address so they can follow up with more information or send you samples?

- What's their history? (Have they expanded their range of products or services? Have they moved out or into markets? Find out why they withdrew from or moved into a market and how that affected their profits.)

- What's their position in the market? (This reflects their 'core value' – our product is the most reliable, for example.)

- What segments are they targeting?

- What distribution channels do they use? (Look at their distributors, sales reps, etc.)

- What is their marketing budget?

22. Find out what your competition is not delivering

Is it something that you could offer? What is something that you can do right now that will fill the gap or offer something that no one else in your industry or area offers? What market category or niche is not being served by your industry? Once you've completed your competitive surveys, begin comparing the data you've collected on your competition with your own operation and use it to identify potential profit-generating opportunities for your company.

23. Define your Unique Selling Proposition

Your Unique Selling Proposition (USP) is the unique position that your company holds in the minds of your potential and existing clients. That position determines whether or not your potential clients will choose to do business with you. A USP is not a catchy slogan – it's crucial to your business success. Without an effective USP, people will never know why they should do business with you.

24. Price is not always a determining factor in purchases

There's a misconception among many business owners that people choose the company that offers the lowest price. This isn't the case – studies have shown that price is seldom the main factor in making a decision to make a purchase. Sometimes offering the cheapest price can be detrimental because potential clients may view your product or service as somehow inferior to others.

There are various ways people define their USP. These can be based on:

- The specific service they provide

- The geographic area they serve

- The demographic group they serve

- The occupations they serve (e.g., marketing consulting for estate agents)

- The career levels of their clients (e.g. CEOs)

- The way they deliver their service (e.g., via the phone or personal meetings)

- The extras they provide

- Their unique qualifications, credentials or experience

25. Your USP must be specific and meaningful to your prospective clients

A USP is also a way of summarising and telegraphing one of the chief benefits of the service being marketed. It's not enough to say "We deliver the best service" or "We offer the best price". That won't set your business apart from your competition. It's not specific, it's not different and consumers hear similar bland statements all the time – it won't motivate them to do business with you. So your USP must be specific. If you deliver the best service in your industry, what does that mean specifically? Quantify your statement. Describe what makes your service unique.

To be successful a company must have a sustainable competitive advantage, something that sets it apart from the competition or makes it unique. What happens if you can't think of anything that is sufficiently unique or different about your company? Then you need to find something that your competition does not offer that creates extra value or that gives clients additional reasons to buy your service. It might even be something that every company in your industry or sector offers as a matter of course but which clients aren't aware of.

The crucial characteristics of an effective USP

- You should be able to define your USP in less than 90 words. And it must describe why people should do business with you and not your competitors. It should therefore capture and reflect the most important source of your competitive advantage.

- It should be memorableIt should be unique.

- It should describe the benefits of your service.

- It must be believable – not challenge people's credence.

- It should be specific about your service quality, selection, etc.

- It should show how your service fills a gap in the market.

- It must be relevant and of importance to your prospects and clients.

- It must be able to evolve to meet your clients' changing needs or wants.

- It must be true. You must be able to deliver what you promise. Never advertise or market a USP that you can't deliver. That will only dent your company's credibility and harm your current and future custom.

26. Don't wait for referrals – ask for them

A referral is someone else doing your sales and marketing for you at no cost and because they want to. Their experience of your service was so positive that they want to share it with other people.

Referrals are the single fastest and easiest way for any business owner to build deep relationships, earn more money, and enjoy the freedom they desire.

Before you ask for referrals ensure that the service you offer is regarded in a positive way by your existing clients. It should delight rather than merely please.

27. Put energy into building a referral programme.

Prospects who are referred are easier to close, make their buying decision faster, are more profitable because there's no cost in acquiring them and they spend/invest more, and they're more loyal – they tend to stay with you longer.

28. Make sure your colleagues and clients know all aspects of your product/service

People talk most about your product/service when they really understand it. But, unfortunately, most clients or customers have usually only experienced the benefit of a few of your skills or one or two of your products. Referrals come faster when clients recognise how you can improve their lives. They must be able to understand all your products/services. They must be able to explain to others what you do. Focus on educating them about all areas of your service and all the products you offer.

29. Dedicate time at the end of each prospect or client meeting to discuss referrals

Many business owners aren't comfortable with the idea of asking for referrals. Overcome this by realising most clients are thrilled that you think so highly of them that you're requesting their help.

30. Continue to build a relationship with clients and colleagues by anticipating their needs

If you want to create top-of-mind awareness in your clients' minds, provide value, and do it fast.

31. Reward referral-generating behaviour

As with any behaviour you want to reinforce, pay attention to and reward referral- generating behaviour. Referrals don't happen just by accident. They are the product of a great client experience, a mix of sales, marketing and client-support efforts. It's too easy to forget to remind clients how great their experience was so that they will be more willing to make further referrals. Out of sight is definitely out of mind, in this case.

Identify the 'ideal' referral candidates, articulate your company's USP and how it relates to their network, create the ideal environment for referrals, and thank the referrers.

32. Generate tons of referrals by doing something extraordinary

Give people a reason to talk about your business or service. Think of something positive you can do that makes it intrinsically conversation-worthy. It has to be a reason that isn't completely self-serving to you. People won't mind helping you to build your business if they have had a good experience but they're not going to go out of their way to do it. Why should they?

33. How you ask for referrals makes all the difference

The art of getting lots of referrals lies in the way you ask for them. If you say, "Do you know anyone else who might enjoy my service?" people will say they'll have a think and let you know. The chances are they will forget the question once they've left your premises, put down the phone or closed your email. So be specific and be direct. Ask, 'Who do you think will benefit from my service?' When they tell you, ask them specifically where you can find those people (their company, industry, or within the organisations, clubs, groups or networks they belong to).

To apply for a free implementation session **worth £495** where we show you how everything in this book can be done for you, go to completedigitalmarketingsystem.com/121

34. Become a preferred service provider

Contact various companies and organisations who deal with your kind of ideal clients and see if you can be set up as a preferred provider of your service. Each company or organisation will recommend you to their employees or clients in exchange for a fee or a commission on every sale you make as a result of their recommendation.

35. Use public speaking to reach a bigger audience

One of the best ways to create a lasting impression on a decision-maker is to deliver your service to them. Of course, you can't normally do that until they've heard of you, so the next best way to demonstrate your expertise is to deliver content in a non-sales setting such as a conference speech, a seminar presentation or in a workshop environment. By listening to your speech or presentation, the decision-maker is highly likely to form an impression about whether they want to work with you or not.

Public speaking – giving lectures, talks, papers, and presentations at public events, industry meetings, conventions, and conferences – is a PR technique that businesses use widely to promote their products or services.

36. Look for speaking opportunities

Unless you're sponsoring your own seminar or other event, you need to find appropriate forums to which you can be invited to speak. How? Check your mail and the trade publications you read for announcements of industry meetings and conventions. Trade journals generally run preview articles and announcements of major shows, expos, and meetings months before the events. Many trade publications also have columns that announce such meetings on both a national and a local level. Make sure to scan these columns in the publications aimed at your target market industries.

You should also receive preview announcements in the mail and via email. Professional societies and trade associations will send you direct-mail packages inviting your firm to exhibit at their shows.

Find out whether papers, talks, or seminars are being given at the show and, if so, get on the panel or signed up as a speaker.

Propose topics. Most conference managers welcome such proposals because they need speakers.

37. Recycle your talks

You can recycle your talks and deliver them to different groups in the same year or different years, tailoring them slightly to fit current market conditions, the theme of the meeting, or the group's special interests. When you create a description, outline, or proposal for a talk, keep it as a file on your computer. Then when other speaking opportunities come your way, you can quickly edit the file and email a customised proposal or abstract to the person in charge of that meeting.

38. Organise any presentation for maximum impact

If your presentation is to be primarily informational, you can organise it along the following lines:

- An introduction that presents an overview of the topic

- The body of the talk, which presents the facts in detail

- A conclusion that sums up for the audience what they've heard

This repetition is beneficial because, unlike readers of an article, listeners of a spoken presentation can't flip back to a previous page or paragraph to refresh their memory or study your material in more detail. For this reason, you must repeat your main point at least three times to make sure that it's understood and remembered.

39. Begin a talk with questions

One easy and proven technique to begin a talk or presentation is to get the audience involved by asking questions. Asking a question has two benefits:

- It provides a quick survey of audience concerns, interests, and levels of involvement, allowing you to tailor your talk to their needs on the spot.

- It forces the audience to become immediately involved. After all, when you're in the audience and the speaker asks a question, you do one of two things: you either do or don't raise your hand. Either way, you're thinking, responding, and getting involved.

40. Don't go over your allotted presentation time

Don't exceed the allotted time for your speech. If you're given 20 minutes with an additional 10 minutes for questions and answers, stop after 20 minutes. People won't mind if you finish a bit early, but they will become fidgety and start looking at their watches if your time limit is up and you don't seem even near finished.

41. Offer a handout with your presentation

A handout can take one of several formats: hard copy of the presentation or slides, brochures, article reprints, or reprints of the narration (with visuals incorporated, if possible). It can be the full text of your talk, an outline, just the visuals, or a report or article on a topic that is either related to the presentation topic or expands on one of the subtopics you touched on briefly in the talk. Every handout should contain your company name, address, phone, fax, website address, email address, and, if possible, a full resource box with a brief summary of who you are and what you do – as should every marketing document you produce.

42. Offer a transcript of the speech after your talk, not before

Handouts such as transcripts of a speech, articles, reports, or other materials with lots of copy should be handed out after the talk, not before. If you hand them out before you step to the podium, the audience will read the printed materials and ignore you. You can hand out reproductions of visuals or pages with just a few bullet points in advance so that attendees can write notes directly on them.

To apply for a free implementation session **worth £495** where we show you how everything in this book can be done for you, go to **completedigitalmarketingsystem.com/121**

23

43. Let your audience know you'll be giving a handout

If the handout is the full text of your talk or a set of fairly comprehensive notes, tell the audience before you start, "There's no need to take notes. We have hard copies of this presentation for you to take home." This relieves listeners of the burden of note taking, freeing them to concentrate on your talk.

44. Avoid boring your audience to death with PowerPoint or slides

Prepare visuals that you can show briefly and then put away. If you use slides or PowerPoint, turn off the projector and turn on the lights when the visuals are not in use. If you do use slides, make them bold, bright, colourful, and easy to read. Use them to show, demonstrate, and create excitement. Don't use them to transmit complex detail. Too much detail in a slide or overhead makes it unclear.

45. Test the readability of a slide before your presentation

Hold the slide at arm's length. If you can't read the text, your audience won't be able to either.

46. Capture attendee names for your prospect database

If the conference organiser won't release a list of attendees or the people who go to your specific session, offer your handout or a free information guide as a bait piece instead of giving it out at the session. At the conclusion of your talk, discuss your handout or information guide and what it covers and say, "So if you'd like a copy of this free report/information guide, just write on the back of your business card and hand it to me. I'll email a free copy to you as soon as I get back to the office." The more enticing and relevant your bait piece, the more business cards you'll collect.

47. Become a dynamic networker

Besides referrals, decision-makers tend to choose service providers they are aware of. That means you must raise your profile to become known to as many decision-makers in your market as possible. One of the easiest ways to raise your profile is through networking.

People want to do business with people they like and trust. Use a networking event as an opportunity to get to know people better and find out how you can help them grow their business. Your networking will be successful once you start looking at it as a way to help others.

48. Mentally rehearse your success at a future networking event

Each day before a networking event, take a few moments to imagine yourself there. Think of it like a movie playing inside your mind: 'see' yourself looking confident, smiling and meeting lots of interesting people, and 'hear' yourself sounding confident and talking with ease. Make the mental picture as vivid as possible. Keep doing it until you have a completely positive 'movie' in your mind.

49. Rehearse your 'elevator pitch'

Your 'elevator pitch' is a one-sentence summary of what your business is about and how it can help your prospects. It's what you could say about your business in the time it would take to get from the ground floor to the top floor in a lift. It should break the ice and start a conversation flowing.

50. Decide on your goals for every networking event

What is your purpose for attending a particular event? Is it: to meet certain people, to find prospective clients, to find a resource you need, to make a new friend, or to nurture existing relationships?

51. Check your business cards before a networking event

Ensure your business card accurately describes what you do. People might not remember you, but your card might be enough to get them to phone you. Print on the back of cards. Make your cards memorable.

52. Pick the right event

If you need to meet plastics manufacturers, for example, find out where they meet and go along. Look up trade associations or check relevant trade media.

53. Research the people who'll be at a networking event

Try to get hold of a list of people who will be at the networking event and look them up. Identify your targets so you can bring some focus to the event.

54. Arrive early to networking events

If you arrive early, the number of people will be smaller and more manageable.

55. Look positive at networking events

Enter the room with a smile. No matter how nervous you feel and however much you might be quaking inside, do your best to appear confident. Breathe! When you meet someone, smile and shake hands firmly. Make lots of eye contact (but not in an unblinking, scary kind of way). If you have a smile on your face, people will see you as approachable, enthusiastic and friendly.

56. Work the room at a networking event

It's too easy to stay talking with friends or colleagues but make the effort to meet new people. Make sure you mingle. Move around. Spend no more than 5-6 minutes talking with any one person.

57. Ask your host to introduce you to people

If the networking event has a greeting committee or ambassadors, find out who they are and ask for help with introductions. Reach out to people standing by themselves and introduce people to each other.

58. Ask open-ended questions

This means questions that ask who, what, where, when, and how rather than those that can be answered with a simple 'yes' or 'no'. This form of questioning opens up the discussion and shows listeners that you are interested in them.

59. Don't hard sell at networking events

Forget trying to 'sell' your business or using the event as a hard-sell opportunity – it's very off-putting. There's nothing worse than a pushy salesperson trying to sell you something at a networking event. Use the opportunity to sound out potential leads, not convert them.

60. Follow up with the people you meet at networking events

When you return to the office, be sure to write out information on the back of the card or a sheet of paper that can be stapled to the card. This way you can maintain and build rapport for a future meeting, email, or phone call.

61. Drop an email to the four or five people you meet at events

Don't blanket email everyone who was there – they won't appreciate it! It's also good to mention a detail you remember and suggest that they keep in touch with you. If there's an obvious win-win connection with someone you've met at an event, call them up and invite them to lunch to explore the connection further.

62. Write winning proposals

A great proposal can help you to win a contract while a poorly written one can undermine all the hard work you've put into forming a relationship with a prospective client. What constitutes a poor proposal? One that's filled with meaningless jargon, looks like a template, arrives late, or doesn't address the client's specific needs. A great proposal should summarise the results you'll provide over what time frame and at what cost.

When you write a proposal, exclude any empty phrases such as 'seamless integration'. Use words, terms and phrases a prospective client will understand immediately.

Only agree to send a proposal when you understand what your prospective client wants and you know how to address those wants. Be aware (even if the client is not) of the underlying cause of the problem.

63. Keep your proposal as brief as possible

Clients tend to select the shortest proposal to read first.

Your proposal must include the following:

- An executive summary.

This should demonstrate your understanding of the client's issues and describe the results you will deliver.

- Background information

This should briefly describe why you have been asked to submit a proposal.

- Objectives

This is where you describe how you will deliver the results you are promising.

- Results

This is where you explain in detail the results you will deliver to your prospective client. Give specific outcomes, results, and time frames.

- Project approach

This explains how you will achieve the results you promise. Explain how the work will be carried out and include the responsibilities of both yourself and your prospective client. Include details of the activities involved as well as the tools and strategies you'll use.

- The team

If you're working with other people, provide details of who they are and how each will contribute to the results you're promising to achieve.

- The schedule

This is where you provide details of how long each phase of the project will take. Do include details of how you will keep the project on time.

- Fees

This is where you provide details of your fees, perhaps even with a range of pricing options depending upon the results you're being asked to deliver. Specify how you expect to be paid (an upfront fee, periodic payments during the project and a project completion fee, for example).

- Qualifications

This is where you explain why a client should use your services. Explain how you've worked through similar challenges with other companies and how you resolved them. Emphasise each of the unique qualities that you will bring to the project and how each will help ensure a successful outcome. Provide case studies and testimonials that demonstrate your expertise at solving clients' problems.

64. Offer prospective clients a huge incentive to make contact with you

Get clients coming to you by offering them a huge incentive to take action. What are the kinds of offers and promotions that would stimulate a list of prospects to get in touch with you?

- Time limited – phone today

- Claim something free

- Add in a bonus gift

- A special offer

- A buy one, get one free promotion

- Something that's running out

What you're looking for is a promotion that creates action NOW – rather than later.

65. Make your sales letters (both offline and online) work hard for you

To be effective, your sales letter must incorporate the following elements:

- An attention-grabbing headline

If you can't grab your prospect's attention you'll lose before you even begin.

Use a subhead to introduce another big benefit or hint at the offer itself, assuming it's especially compelling. If the headline is an outrageous claim then you can use the subhead to validate your headline.

- The body

Identify the problem. Gain your prospect's attention by identifying a problem that resonates with them. Once you've identified the pain, agitate it (rub salt in the wound). Overcome their inertia: remind people of their pain over and over again if you want them to take action.

Use bullet points.

Use social proof.

- The Offer

Elements of effective offers

Open with a "reason why" you're making the offer. Vividly show the value of each element of your offer. Use images. Reveal the price but show how it pales in comparison to the overall value your product/ service delivers. Pile on bonuses they will want so the offer becomes truly irresistible. Discuss the payment terms (i.e. split-pay, free-trial, etc.) if applicable

You must eliminate your prospect's ability to procrastinate, because they will if left alone. Scarcity can be accomplished in three ways:

i) Limited Quantity

ii) Price increase (date or quantity driven)

iii) Loss of a valuable bonus

To apply for a free implementation session **worth £495** where we show you how everything in this book can be done for you, go to **completedigitalmarketingsystem.com/121**

- Call to action

Don't assume your prospect knows what to do next... you need to tell them! Be explicit and succinct in your instructions.

66. Test putting the call to action in multiple places in the sales letter

Don't just place your call to action at the bottom of your sales letter. Some common places for the call to action include:

- Beneath testimonials

- After the bonuses

- In the P.S.

- At the top of the letter

67. Paint a vivid picture of what will happen if people don't take action

Remind people of the dire consequences of not taking action – of how much more painful the problem will become.

68. Always include a P.S.

Every sales letter you write should include at least one P.S. (and most will include two or even three – the first being a warning of what will happen if they miss out, the second a recap of the offer and benefits, and the third a trust-building phrase or sentence). The P.S. is the third most important element of most sales letters (behind the headline and first paragraph)...use it wisely!

Use it to:

- Restate the primary benefits

- Restate the scarcity component

- Make at least one additional call to action

69. Test your P.S.

If your prospects only read the headline and the P.S., would it give them enough information to make them want to buy? If not, rewrite it.

70. Form strategic alliances

A strategic alliance is an easy way to explore new market opportunities, find new leads, attract new clients and really turbo-boost your sales BUT careful planning is imperative because they do involve time, resources and energy.

Why form a strategic alliance? They allow your business to gain a competitive edge through access to a partner's resources – whether they are markets, technologies, capital or people. With a strategic alliance, you increase your resources and capabilities which in turn boost your company's growth and expansion. You may gain access to more established channels of distribution, marketing or branding.

71. Consider forming a strategic alliance with your competitors to share your unconverted leads

People mistakenly assume that every other company in their industry is a competitor. But they're not. You can share similar client bases but just because someone hired you rather another service provider doesn't mean they hate the other person and love you. It means that:

- The timing was right
- The price was right.

72. Define your outcome before forming a strategic alliance

Decide what you want from the relationship: access to a market, new clients, or ways to retain your existing clients.

73. Be aware of why strategic alliances fail

One of the biggest reasons for failure in strategic alliances is an incompatibility between company cultures. The ideal partner in a strategic alliance is one that has resources, skills and assets that complement your own. The strategic alliance has to work contractually, but there should also be a good fit between the cultures of the two organisations.

74. Define how the strategic alliance will operate

How will the partnership work? Will you or the other company help each other to become more efficient, will the other company bundle your product with their offering, or will they sell your product on a commission? Ensure that the relationship works financially for both you and your partner. Unless you both gain from the partnership, one of you will lack motivation and feel resentful and the relationship will crumble.

75. Don't tie the deal up with so many clauses that neither of you has room to move

Do have an exit strategy in place should either of you decide to dissolve the strategic alliance. Strategic alliance partnerships may take time and energy to set up and run but they can also make a huge difference to your company's bottom line.

76. Generate free publicity to get more leads

Public Relations (PR) means you and your business getting coverage (being written about in the media or being featured on the radio or TV). PR is a very effective way of attracting new clients and reminding old clients of your existence, therefore rekindling their interest in your service. And it costs you virtually nothing.

Credibility makes publicity a very valuable tool. People know that advertising is paid for and that companies can buy space to say whatever they wish about their products and services. And for this reason, people are more sceptical today than ever before. One way to get around this scepticism is via publicity – people know it can't be bought; it appears to be endorsed by the medium that makes your announcement. And since people tend to trust the media they watch, listen to, or read regularly, they accept your message as being completely credible.

That's why publicity can win you many more sales than any form of paid advertising or promotion. Taking advantage of this credibility can result in a windfall for your company.

77. Offer press releases to generate publicity

The most common way of getting a story in the media is through a one or two page press release. Media outlets always have their reader/audience in mind so your press release must be angled and written in a way that will appeal to them. You can also send a list of bullet points which cover the salient points of your story.

You could also try calling first to gauge their interest (but check their deadlines before you call – you'll get a much better response if you make contact a long way before the deadline).

78. Offer media outlets news they'll use

In general, information outlets are looking for:

- Topical news releases relating to timely issues. The media is particularly interested in certain trends and your services, no matter what they are, can tie into one of those trends.

- Community involvement releases sponsoring events or get-togethers.

- Industry-specific projections and surveys that predict where a niche market is headed.

Generating news and information that people and the press will be interested in is not as difficult as it may sound. All you have to do is ask, "What does my target audience care about?" It will help to focus your thoughts and ideas. Conducting some research on a specific topic or question will help you get the answer.

79. Use your press releases to send prospects to your website

Place hyperlinks in your press releases that send prospects to the relevant page of your website (or to a specific landing page set up for the PR campaign).

80. Set up a 'media' section on your website

Upload all your press releases onto separate pages of your media section. Google prefers websites that are adding new content and gives them higher rankings in search results. That means more visitors to your web pages.

81. Leverage your publicity

When you get media coverage, share it with everyone you do business with and include it in all your marketing material. If potential clients see that your business is the one that the media is talking about, that's going to give you a significant competitive advantage.

82. Collect and use testimonials

You can attract or 'catch' more clients by collecting testimonials from your clients and using them in your marketing materials (both online and offline). It lets your clients do the talking and convincing for you and your business. If possible, include the client's photograph, their real name, position within their company and location. That way, prospects can see that the testimonials are genuine.

83. Ask clients to provide details in their testimonials

Some testimonials aren't particularly useful: they're the ones that say "Wow! Your company's great!" Ask clients to go into detail about how your service has improved or benefited their company.

For example, someone might go on an investment training course and say: "When I first came on your investment training course I was £5,000 in debt. However, after using the advice I am now £10,000 in credit after paying off all my credit cards. I now have a bright future ahead of me because I know that I'm in control of my financial destiny." Compare that with the run-of-the-mill testimonial that says, "Fantastic!" Which has more credibility?

84. Get a range of testimonials

Have a range of testimonials to endorse what you do from every single angle. Think of it as a CAT scan providing clarity from every single angle and providing absolute transparency so there is no doubt in anyone's mind.

The key is to get testimonials about different aspects of your product or service. If you get a whole range of testimonials saying the same thing it reinforces the point, but ideally what you want to see is them coming from different angles. So have:

- One testimonial saying what great service you provide

- One testimonial saying how easy you are to do business with

- One testimonial talking about the value for money your service provides

- One testimonial talking about the outcome derived from using your service and how it exceeded your clients' expectations

- One testimonial saying how much your clients have recommended your products or service to their friends and family members

- One testimonial saying, "I've tried other companies' services and they don't measure up to yours."

85. Use telemarketing to bring in more business

Although it is often maligned and frequently misunderstood, telemarketing provides an opportunity to make one-to-one contact with the prospective client at a very low cost.

Telemarketing can be used to:

- Expand your current client base

- Improve the monetary amount per sale

- Improve your company's client service image

- Provide an opportunity for follow-up sales

- Generate leads for outside salespeople

- Sell a service directly over the phone

- Provide an incoming service for people to request additional information

86. Use a three-step marketing approach

A one-step marketing approach is attempting to make an immediate sale with an advertisement, sales letter, or other promotion. The prospective client must make an immediate buying decision. He or she must either purchase the product/service or not. If the client decides not to buy and leaves, you have lost the opportunity to develop and nurture an ongoing relationship with them. You've in effect lost not just the first sale but future sales.

A more effective method is to use three steps in the selling process. Step one is to make contact with the prospect and offer valuable information for free in return for their contact details. Step two is to build a relationship with your prospect through regular contact (sales letters and emails) that continue to offer value. Step three is to nurture the relationship until the prospect is comfortable enough with you and your organisation to buy your product/service.

87. Encourage people to climb the marketing ladder

If you want people to buy your service, you must give something away first. Many business owners mistakenly assume that 'window shopping' prospects will be prepared to hire them or buy from them without any prior experience or knowledge of the service being offered but they need much, much more.

You must woo your prospects, offering them low or no cost samples, then something that is a little bit more expensive and so on until they are familiar enough with you and your company to consider your highest priced service. Doing it this way makes purchase decisions easier.

As the relationship between you and your prospect develops, the objections he or she may have had initially begin to disappear.

To apply for a free implementation session **worth £495** where we show you how everything in this book can be done for you, go to **completedigitalmarketingsystem.com/121**

37

To make the process easy, you need to have a range of services at different prices so prospects can gradually move toward the more expensive range at a pace that makes them comfortable.

88. Use back-end and front-end marketing

Once you've overcome your prospects' resistance to buy from you, it's crucial that you continue to nurture the relationship so they keep buying your services. Keep providing them with useful, relevant information and occasionally offering them opportunities to buy more advanced services.

You can boost your sales by also offering up-sell, cross-sell, even down-sell opportunities (if they opt out of one of your more expensive services, you can offer them something cheaper).

89. Create additional products/services to offer first-time buyers

When you offer a better version or supplemental products/services that the client needs in order to benefit more fully from what you're offering, you not only create more cash for yourself, you create a happier client who ultimately enjoys their purchase more.

90. Offer multiple payment methods

People have a strong resistance to buy and it doesn't matter how good your product or service is, you still need to deal with their natural scepticism. You have to overcome their resistance. The more you do to put prospective clients at ease, the more they will buy from you.

An effective way of lessening buyers' resistance is offering multiple payment methods to make it easier to purchase your service. These might include early bird discounts, PayPal, credit or debit cards, bank cheque, payment plans, etc.

Offer enticing bonuses

Any bonuses you offer should be of low cost to you but high perceived value to the client. So, it's important that you when you make the offer, you put a monetary value on the bonuses (for example, 'You'll also receive this special bonus report worth £97 absolutely free and it's yours to keep – no matter what').

91. Reward clients so they keep coming back

Finding first-time clients takes time, money and energy (think of the advertising, direct mail, telemarketing, email marketing, and overhead costs).

Each client you attract and sell can cost as much or more than the profit you make from each sale. Therefore, it makes sense to make additional sales to each client you have already bought and paid for with your marketing efforts.

In the clamour to find new clients, many businesses forget their existing clients. This is a huge and costly mistake: if clients don't feel they are appreciated, they'll move on.

Ignore your existing clients and you miss not only the opportunity to show them how much you really do care about the relationship (and naturally, their purchase and their ongoing business with you) but also to ask for referrals and testimonials.

92. Maintain frequent contact with your clients

Unless clients know what you have to offer and the benefits to them, they simply won't buy. Keep them informed by thanking them for existing business and telling them what you have to offer by letter, newsletter, ezine, phone, email or even personally.

A new service or product is an excellent excuse to contact them. A special thank you discount or exclusive offer to loyal clients is a great way to keep them buying from you.

Make a point of delivering more than clients expect. When you exceed clients' expectations, they will be delighted and feel obligated to return the gesture. They'll refer you to their friends, family and work colleagues and they'll stay your client for longer.

To apply for a free implementation session **worth £495** where we show you how everything in this book can be done for you, go to **completedigitalmarketingsystem.com/121**

39

93. Never ignore your existing customers

Don't overlook the potential of current customers when considering where to focus for growth. Your best prospect is very often your current customer, who knows your brand and would be most open to trying something new from it. Besides, it's cheaper to market to an existing customer than it is to get a new customer.

94. Only focus on markets with growth potential

One of the biggest mistakes marketers make is focusing on a target market that is too small and then setting sales and profit objectives that can't possibly be reached. Be careful about choosing a target market that is shrinking over time or that is too small to allow you to meet sales objectives.

95. Set measurable marketing objectives

Don't set objectives that are not measurable. Make your objectives specific and quantifiable. Marketing objectives fall into one of three categories:

- The retention of existing customers

- To increase the purchase amount from existing customers

- To increase the number of new customers

To effectively manage your marketing function, you will need to know whether you accomplished your objectives or not. If your objectives aren't specific and quantifiable, this will not be possible.

Good objectives are SMART:

- Specific

- Measurable

- Actionable.

- Results-oriented

- Time-specific.

96. Make sure your prices are consistent with your product/service positioning

High prices suggest premium products/services. Low prices suggest bargain products/services. If you want your products or services to be considered high quality, your prices should reflect that. Make sure your sales come from higher price points than the industry or market you operate in.

97. Monitor your competitors' pricing levels

Don't ignore what your competitors are doing price-wise. Your pricing decisions should be based on real market analysis so keep an eye on what they're selling their products or services for.

98. Price sensitivity is affected by brand relevance and brand differentiation

If the customers purchasing your brand do so because of superior attributes or some other more intangible connection that you've established over time, they will be far less price sensitive. On the other hand, if you have an undifferentiated, parity brand, you will find more price sensitivity and elasticity. In many instances, the more intangible or differentiated your brand, the less price sensitivity exists. Service firms are very good examples of this – clients judge them on intangible factors such as reputation, etc.

99. Understand the demographic trends affecting your business

Demographics are things like:

- Age of consumers

- Income of consumers

- Education level of consumers

- Family composition of consumers, such as female-headed household, number of people per household, presence of children, and number of children

- Ethnicity of consumers.

Consumer trends provide another level of insight into consumer demand that can help you make smart decisions about whom to market to and what products your business should market.

100. Understand your competition

Good marketers have a solid understanding of their competitors and their strengths and weaknesses. It would be foolhardy for a small company to take a well-entrenched, well-resourced competitor head on.

Monitor both your primary and secondary competitors. All businesses have a primary and secondary set of competitors. It is helpful to define the key competitors with whom you compete–those that are most like you and serve the same customer profile, with the same shopping intent, with the same channel, with roughly the same price and product categories.

Chapter 2

Website Mistakes

In a Nutshell

Your website has the potential to sell your products or services on your behalf 24 hours a day, seven days a week. Unfortunately, a lot of small and medium-sized businesses make easily avoidable website mistakes, and this potential is not realised. You need to act on this and you need the support to do so.

An all too common scenario is that your website is so riddled with mistakes that it's frustrating and annoying to visitors who leave as soon as they can. That means for every day that it's online, it's probably costing you money in lost sales and lost referrals as well as causing untold damage to your company's reputation.

Worse, you may not realise the mistakes that it contains.

If you recognise any of the following mistakes, take action immediately so that your website can at last deliver the results it is meant to. All of these mistakes stop you getting more customers so you must resolve them now.

101. Not having a way to capture leads

If your website doesn't have an opt-in box, you have no way of collecting the names and contact details of the people who visit your website and don't buy your product or book your service. This oversight will almost certainly cost your company a huge amount of money in terms of lost sales and lost referrals because you won't have any way of getting in contact with them once they leave.

To apply for a free implementation session **worth £495** where we show you how everything in this book can be done for you, go to **completedigitalmarketingsystem.com/121**

43

102. Believing prospective clients care about your website

No one cares about your website. They really don't. They couldn't care less that your website goal is to boost sales by 25% or to open a new marketing channel. And why should they? The only care they have when they arrive on your website is solving their problem as quickly as possible. Most people visit a website to solve one or more of these four problems:

- They want/need information

- They want/need to make a purchase /donation

- They want/need to be entertained

- They want/need to be part of a community.

103. Not organising your website categories for your users

Being mysterious, tricky, or ironic with your website's category labels is a huge mistake online. When choosing names for the categories on your website, keep your audience's expectations in mind. Use terms they're familiar with. Make sure the terms you use match the content within categories. Your audience and their goals (not yours) should determine the method of categorisation you use.

104. Looking like your competitors' websites

Don't slavishly copy the websites of your competitors. Your website should stand out in your marketplace, not blend in. If it looks like your competitors' websites, you're not going to be able to steal any of their business. Instead, your prospective clients will be confused. 'Me too' companies rarely win. Plus, when people are given too many options, they tend to dismiss those that appear to be the same. You need to ensure that your website (and in fact your business overall) is clearly differentiated from your competition.

105. Distracting people from buying by putting links in their way

Once visitors have started along the path to make a purchase or a booking, you'll sabotage the sale if you distract them from completing the purchase or booking. Don't throw irrelevant links in their path that will distract them or waste their time. Other obstacles that get in the way of a sale include: splash pages, flash splash pages (video), animations, lack of a focal point on the page, too much text, too little text and too many pictures. It's crazy! Make it easy for visitors to do what they came to your site to do.

106. Not having a plan to drive traffic to your website

It's not enough to create a website – you have to let people know that it exists. You need a plan to drive traffic to your website. That plan must have at least a few different ways to get traffic. That's because it's dangerous to rely on a single method of attracting website visitors. If that method became less effective, you would have no other way of getting traffic to your site.

There are many ways to drive traffic. You can optimise your website to perform better in Google searches. That is effective but it can take a long time to work. A faster way to get traffic is to advertise using pay per click (PPC) advertising such as Google AdWords. The beauty of this is that you don't pay until you get the traffic, as you only pay when people click the advert. You can also send email broadcasts, generate links from other websites, use online and offline PR, and offline methods such as postcard marketing and advertising in publications.

107. Not answering the questions your visitors arrive with.

Website visitors look at your website and want answers to their very specific questions. Those questions are:

- Is this site credible?

- Is it trustworthy?

- Is this a professional company?

- Is this company stable?

- Does this site make me feel welcome?

- Am I in the right place?

The elements on your homepage or landing page must convey that your website is credible, trustworthy, and owned by a professional, stable and reliable company. It must also reassure your visitors that it has the information, product or service they're looking for.

108. Not telling people what your website is about

Visitors spend a few seconds (no more than about eight) looking to decide whether a website has anything of interest to them. If it doesn't, they leave and go to another website. If your website doesn't convey what it is about, your visitors will leave and probably never return.

That means you lose the opportunity to ever foster a relationship with that visitor to encourage them to buy from you. It also means you never get the opportunity to encourage them to refer their colleagues, contacts or friends to your business.

109. Trying to make the sale too soon

Although your website exists to sell your products or services, it's a huge mistake to bombard visitors with hard-sell messages from the moment they arrive. It's the equivalent of unleashing a crowd of bombastic, pushy salespeople on them. They'll just want to escape as quickly as possible.

110. Not optimising your website for mobile web browsers

People using mobile web browsers will scan your webpages much more than if they were using a desktop browser. Of course, scanning a page is the typical way of consuming web page content on a desktop anyway but based on the fact that, for example, many smart phone users will be looking for a quick hit of information or to kill a little time, the ease with which the relevant points of your text stand out, the better chance your content has of achieving the desired effect

111. Not telling people what you want them to do

Once you have grabbed someone's attention with a compelling headline and explained the benefits and features of your product or service in the webpage (this is what builds their interest and desire), you need to force them to take action. That can be as simple as putting at the bottom of each web page the action you would like them to take. "Ring us now for the latest prices" or "click here to book now".

What you don't want to do is allow that person to put off taking action because they will most likely forget about your offer once their attention is diverted by something else. An intended future purchase is no good for your business. You want sales or bookings now!

To motivate your prospective buyer to take immediate action there are a number of proven influential elements that you can build into your offer. The simplest is to build in some kind of scarcity. For example, if you were to write next to your action trigger that there are only seven of these products left, then you'll see some interesting results.

Those people who are interested will be forced to ask themselves a question. If there are only seven of these items left, then they have to make an immediate decision. "Will I regret it if I don't get my hands on one of the last seven?" they will ask themselves. By 'forcing' prospects to make an immediate decision in this way you are much more likely to see positive purchasing decisions.

If you don't have limited stocks of something, then add a different kind of scarcity. The ability to buy an item at half the normal price – but only until Friday – forces your potential client to make a decision about how badly they want it.

112. Not catering to website 'browsers'

Research has shown that most visitors to websites can be classified into two groups: they are either 'hunters' (the people who know what they want and are simply looking for the easiest, quickest and most secure way to get it) or they are 'browsers' (they are the people who are doing the equivalent of 'window-shopping': they're having a quick look at your website in search of the answers to their problem or challenge).

The browsers, who most likely make up the majority of your website visitors, are on your website to learn and to find answers

To apply for a free implementation session **worth £495** where we show you how everything in this book can be done for you, go to **completedigitalmarketingsystem.com/121**

47

to the questions they have. Those questions are like barriers to them making a booking or buying something from you. If you don't answer their questions, those barriers are left in place and stop them from booking or buying anything. They will leave and probably never return. Instead, they'll go to your competitors' websites.

113. Not catering to website hunters

Hunters, one of the two groups of website visitors, arrive on your website with a clear idea of what they want. They're simply there to find the easiest, quickest and most secure way to get it. Hunters need to be led quickly to what they came for and you need to eliminate any elements that might distract them from their initial objective – to buy products from you.

To convince hunters that your website is where they should make the purchase, it must answer the questions hunters typically have:

- Is this the place?

- Where is the thing I want?

- Is this the best price/quality I can get?

- Is it really safe to buy from this site?

114. Allowing content to get stale

As busy as you and everyone else in your company undoubtedly are, you mustn't allow the content on your website to get stale. Out of date information on your website is a way of announcing to the world at large that "We're disorganised here and not very reliable". It's like leaving an 'Out to lunch' sign outside your office for a few months. Make sure that your website carries current information, particularly on your blog, news pages, and events pages.

115. Filling the website with content about you and your company

It's a harsh truth but website visitors are not interested in your company. They don't lie awake at night wondering what your company philosophy really is. They don't arrive on your website desperate to know the *real* story behind your new company headquarters. They actually don't want to read about you (until they decide to buy from you, they don't care about you...). That's why your website should not shout "me, me, me". It should be filled with information that potential clients will consider to be highly valuable.

Your website content needs to tell prospects how your service or product will fix their problem or make them feel good. It needs to educate them about their intended purchase.

Make sure your content is written for them and is not just about you. Put yourself in the shoes of your prospect and try to think the way they do. Why have they visited your website? Why are they interested in your solution? What questions are they likely to have? When you think that way, you can then write content that answers their questions, and presents whatever you sell as the answer.

116. Using poorly written copy

You can't just plonk any old words on your website and hope for the best. The text on your website needs to be carefully crafted so that it interests then persuades your visitors to take the action you want them to take – whether that's signing up for a free information guide, emailing or calling you to book an appointment or buying your products.

To do that, you need to use copy that sells. The most effective form of sales copy follows the AIDA Formula – Attention, Interest, Desire, and Action, always in that order. The AIDA acronym helps to focus on the key actions you want your prospective clients to take: attention, interest, desire, and action.

To get people's **attention**, headlines are crucially important. Online, you've got less than eight seconds to grab people's attention before they leave and go to another website. To capture readers' **interest**, use details in the content that they will be able to relate to. Those details can include facts, stories, anecdotes, etc. The copy needs to answer every reader's unspoken question: What's in it for me? The copy must interest and relate to your reader, not to your company.

To apply for a free implementation session **worth £495** where we show you how everything in this book can be done for you, go to **completedigitalmarketingsystem.com/121**

49

To create **desire** for your service in your readers, use power words that trigger excitement and convey a mood.

You then need to tell your reader to take **action** so they can receive the benefits you've highlighted. Let them know the benefit of taking action and the pain they'll experience if they don't take action. It's important to tell them exactly what action they need to take.

117. Not actually telling people what service or product you provide

It's very easy to become so blinkered about your company and your industry or market that you forget that other people don't actually know or understand what it is you do. Look at your website from an outsider's perspective and see whether it's really easy to tell from the content and images what your company is offering.

118. Not measuring your website's performance

You need to test and measure your website so that you have all the information you need to make refinements that will improve its effectiveness. The things you should measure are:

- Conversion rate: The number of visitors to your website that become paying customers

- Visitor value: That's how much each visitor spends

- Opt-in sign-up rate: How many visitors are giving you their contact information

- Traffic statistics: How many visitors does your website attract?

- Traffic source: Which traffic generators are driving traffic to your website?

- Average visit time: How long does a visitor stay on your website?

- Most viewed site pages: Which pages attract the most visitors?

- Traffic stats – what is the number of visitors?

- Source of visitors – what traffic generators are bringing you prospects?

- Average visit time – how long does a visitor stay onsite?

- Most-viewed site pages – which pages are drawing eyes?

119. Not testing your website to find out what's missing or not working

Observe, monitor and interview your website users to discover if your website is missing some vital information or needs improving in any way. Ask them for areas or processes they would like to see improved. Test it yourself, particularly the links and online buying process. And if you ask people for their opinion and/or advice, take action and fix what's broken or missing. Once you've done it, let them know by email when you've taken action to remedy the situation they highlighted.

120. Offering a website that's slow to load

Visitors are very impatient and so will only give your website at the very most five seconds to load. If it takes longer than that, they will go. And they will take with them your opportunity to turn them into a paying client.

121. Using boring descriptions for products or services

Boring product and service descriptions are a big turn-off. If you want to hold your visitors' attention, use a USP-driven, benefit-rich description of your products or services and then provide a 'read more' link to all pertinent data and specifications.

You can't grab and hold people's attention for any length of time with "plain vanilla" product specifications. While all pertinent data and specs should be accessible through a link, a benefit-rich, USP-driven sales message should be the first thing a visitor sees when he/she arrives at your site.

To apply for a free implementation session **worth £495** where we show you how everything in this book can be done for you, go to **completedigitalmarketingsystem.com/121**

51

122. Using stock keeping units instead of words to describe products

It may be convenient for you to label your product by its stock keeping unit (SKU) '#3423-0002-345' rather than 'all-weather leather work boot with steel cap toes and lambswool lining', but it will do absolutely nothing for your sales. You need to convince people to buy your products and the SKU just won't do it. If you're at a loss to describe your products in an enticing way, hire a professional catalogue copywriter to do it for you.

123. Making it difficult to contact you

Really, the only excuse you have for making it difficult for website visitors to get in contact with you is if you're a fugitive from the law. You must make it really easy for visitors to get in contact with you and your team, especially if you're selling products online or offering downloadable products. That's because people will have questions that they expect to have answered immediately (or at least within 24 hours). If they can't get in contact with you, they'll assume that you're on the run and your business is completely dodgy. Understandably, they'll leave in search of a company that is transparent, trustworthy and legitimate.

124. Using complex navigation

Complex navigation can be confusing and even intimidating for website visitors, especially if the navigation bars have not only drop down menus but also sub menus. It's best to offer a limited number of options on navigation bars (no more than 10 options). Keep the navigation bars in the same position throughout the website too.

125. Not offering anything to encourage sign-ups

You need to give visitors an incentive to hand over their contact details to you. The offer of a free newsletter was once enough to entice even the most cynical web visitor to give you a name and email address but that is no longer the case. Your offer needs to be something that your visitors really want and consider worth having like an information guide or software trial.

126. Not using visual hierarchy on your web pages

One very common design mistake is poor visual hierarchy – not giving importance to the most important elements of the content of your web pages. If your visitors don't see information prioritised in a certain way, they won't take an action that you want them to take on your website. The result will then be higher bounce rates and poor conversion rates.

Visual hierarchy means giving visual clues as to the most important elements on any web page. You should plan content that progresses and is arranged in a way that your visitors will be mostly likely to be engaged with. Well-constructed hierarchy pulls your visitors' attention toward elements that you want them to pay attention to.

Some visual cues are:

- Size

- Colour

- Contrast

- Shape

- Position

- White space

A great example of visual hierarchy that is used on just about every website is headings (h1, h2, h3, etc.) which indicate importance of information and are usually styled in such a way that they visually guide a visitor from h1 (most important) down to the least important content.

Most written Western languages are read left to right and top to bottom. Also, centred information is more important visually than information at the edges. This means that if you want something to be seen and acted on, you need to place it in the centre of people's field of vision. The natural direction of reading also indicates that content on the right is more noticeable than content on the left of the page. An element that the visitor must see should be somewhere in the centre third of the page and preferably to the right.

To apply for a free implementation session **worth £495** where we show you how everything in this book can be done for you, go to **completedigitalmarketingsystem.com/121**

53

Colour and text attributes. Colour, font styles such as bold or underlined, and font size send a message of importance and hierarchy.

127. Not using a short or memorable domain name

Your domain name needs to be short and memorable. Avoid using domain names that are too long (for example, **www.davidsmithcomputerrepairsabergavenny.com**). Your domain needs to be memorable so avoid names that can't be remembered or spelt easily (for example, **www.scentsandinscentsability.com**). Also avoid names that can't be heard easily over the phone (for example, **www.phosphorescenceessentials.co.uk**).

128. Not bothering to carry out website maintenance

One of the most frustrating experiences for website visitors is to click on a link and to be taken to a page that says something like, "Oops… that page no longer exists". It's the equivalent of opening the door of a five-star hotel room to discover the bed hasn't been made or going for a meal at a restaurant and finding the table hasn't been wiped down. Nothing says "This company can't be bothered" quite like a broken link because it shows you don't carry out regular site maintenance. And quite rightly, your website visitors will assume that there must be other things you can't be bothered doing – like keeping the website secure, checking that your products are safe and that your services are up-to-date. This stuff really does matter so make sure you carry out regular site maintenance.

129. Not featuring your company name prominently on your homepage

You need to place your company name and logo on your homepage so that visitors can see at a glance who owns the site. This will also help to clarify in their mind what your website's purpose is.

130. Using meaningless slogans to convey the value your product or service provides

You need to tell people specifically the value your product or service will deliver. Don't use meaningless phrases such as "We're there for you when you can't be" because your visitors won't have a clue what it means. If you confuse them, they'll leave.

131. Using your Mission Statement on your website

Website visitors won't give two hoots about your Mission Statement so don't waste valuable space on your website with it.

132. Not using testimonials on your website

Testimonials are a very powerful marketing tool and can help to convert website visitors by showing them that other people have bought your products or services and been thrilled and that they've found your customer service to be outstanding. That helps persuade your visitors that the fears they may have about signing up for your blog or free information guide, buying your products or booking your service, are unfounded.

133. Not giving full names of people with their testimonials

Although 'J. Smith from Wiggin' absolutely raved about your products or services in his testimonial, it is a mistake to use his testimonial on your website. That's because a testimonial that doesn't provide the full name of the person who wrote it looks fake. If some of your customers have written testimonials and given only their initial, contact them and ask if you can use their full name instead.

134. Not giving testimonials enough prominence on your website

It's important that all your visitors see your testimonials because they provide valuable social proof that others have used your service and been delighted with it. People are inherently sceptical about the claims a company makes in its advertising but they do pay attention to what other people say about the company.

If you don't place testimonials where people will see and possibly read them, your testimonials won't be able to work their magic and dispel the fears those people might have about your products, services or company. So those website visitors will leave without ever knowing how much your customers think of your products or service, or about your customer service. And they probably won't return. Instead, they'll go to your competitors' websites.

You need to place your testimonials where they will be seen and read by most website visitors. Since many people will explore no further than the first screen of your homepage or any other web page, there's no point burying them beyond the first screen of a web page. You should have a dedicated 'Testimonials' page and lay the testimonials out so they are easy to read. You should also use some of the best testimonials throughout your website copy.

135. Not having a visible cookie policy on your website

All websites in the UK and EU are now required by law to have a visible cookie policy if they serve cookies. A cookie is a very simple text file that gets downloaded from your website onto the PCs of your website visitors. Cookies generally contain the name of a website and a unique user ID. Your site then 'knows' a visitor has been on your site and can use that knowledge to tailor the experience they have. Most commercial websites use cookies.

The EU Cookie Law is designed to protect web users from unwanted marketing and to safeguard their privacy. It means that you must get the consent of web users before serving them with web cookies.

There are two very good reasons for complying: having a cookie policy shows that your company cares about the privacy of the people who visit its website. And the second reason is that the maximum penalty for not complying with the EU 'Cookie Law' is £500,000 for cases where there is a deliberate breach of the law that causes substantial distress. There are also smaller penalties such as being sent an information notice or an enforcement notice.

136. Using text that's filled with inconsistencies or errors

The dominance of text on the web makes it important for you to get the text on your website right. If it's riddled with spelling mistakes, grammatical errors or inconsistencies, that will reflect poorly not only on your website but also on your company and its products or services. That's because it shows that you are a company that is not that bothered about appearances or quality – and you don't mind if things go wrong or look wrong. That's not a reputation that will endear you to prospective clients or customers.

137. Using boring copy

What converts people from looking to buying is relevant content that helps them make a decision to buy from you or to make an enquiry about your product or service. The content needs to make them feel that they have found the solution to their problems: that you can help them or they have found just what they are looking for after hours of searching.

You want to become your target audience's best friend.

Unfortunately, a lot of web copy fails miserably and reads like company Mission Statements –overly wordy, irrelevant to anyone but the writer and utterly boring.

Get professional help: hire a direct mail copywriter to create copy that will convert, rather than bore and repel your prospective clients.

138. Not having follow-up strategies in place

As soon as a visitor signs up to receive your free offer (whatever it may be), they should receive an email in their inbox, confirming they've requested something from your website. Once they confirm their request, they should then receive an email from you that thanks them for their interest and gives them a download link so they get can their hands on the free offer. Using an automated email service (an autoresponder) makes this follow up very easy for you because it delivers a series of emails to your prospective clients or customers over a series of weeks or even months.

139. Using fonts that are difficult to read

Avoid using fonts that are difficult to read. Visitors will click away rather than struggle to read them.

140. Conveying the wrong image for your company

Your website must reflect your company's image so make sure all the elements that you use convey that image. If your company is conservative, for example, the colours, images and text should convey that.

141. Using distracting pop-ups, banners and links on your webpages

Using links, banners, and pop-ups for affiliate programmes and other profit streams can distract your website visitors and keep them from your main goal: to buy a product from you or book your service. You don't have to do away with them completely, but do limit yourself.

142. Going overboard with graphics and animation

Many web developers can't help but try to convince you that your website would be so much better if only it featured animation and graphics. However, tests have shown that too many graphics can have a negative effect on the user experience. Avoid using anything that makes your website slow to load – people will very quickly lose patience and move on to another website.

143. Using weird categories on your website

Don't try to be clever or innovative with the way in which you categorise content on your website. You'll just confuse and annoy your prospective customers or clients if you use 'funny' or illogical categories.

What happens when you frustrate or annoy your visitors? They hit the back button in search of a website that doesn't waste their time or confuse them. Make sure your content categories are organised in a hierarchical, mutually exclusive, sensible way. So, for example, don't replace the traditional 'About Us' page category with something like 'About You'. It will just baffle your visitors.

144. Giving inadequate product or service descriptions.

The information you give about your product or service should help people decide if it's something they want to buy or order. Using a phrase like "Brand New!" or "Bigger than Ever" won't clinch the sale because it doesn't tell your prospective customers anything of value. Provide honest descriptions of what your product or service does and does not do. Describe the benefits and features of the service or product in a way that will appeal to your target market.

145. Not testing your product or service categories on representative users.

Don't just ask people within your company whether the categories you've chosen for your website are logical and useful because that's about as useful as asking your mum if your company is any good. The response you get will almost certainly be biased. You need to test your categories in the real marketplace, even if it means your ideas are shot down in flames. Ask a group of people from your target market to look at the category names. Find out if the categories mean to them what you intend them to mean. If they are confused by the category names or misinterpret them, you and your designers, not your customers, have got it wrong and the names have to be changed.

146. Overusing your keywords on a webpage

Repeating your primary keywords loads of times on individual webpages in the belief it will help nab you a top spot on search engines is a massive mistake. Do not use your main keywords more than three times on a webpage.

147. Putting huge slabs of text on a webpage

One of the top 10 web design mistakes is to use great blocks of copy on your web pages. It just slows people down or repels them. Website visitors are usually in a hurry. They have short attention spans. They scan webpages for a couple of seconds and decide there and then if it's something they can be bothered with. If they're confronted by a solid wall of text, they'll think it looks boring and will take too long to plough through. They'll hit the 'back' button and leave. You need to make the text look quick and easy to read. Web design author Steve Krug suggests you "get rid of half of the words on each page then get rid of half of what's left."

148. Not making your text scannable

Visitors scan webpages for words and pictures that match their goals. They are looking to see if it contains anything of interest. Make your text scannable by using subheadings, bulleted lists, and short paragraphs. Highlight keywords.

149. Using white text on a dark background

White text is very difficult to read, especially online. Use dark (black or blue) text on a light background to make it easy for your website visitors to read.

150. Not answering visitors' questions

Website visitors arrive on your site to accomplish something – to find out answers to their questions, or to buy a product or book a service. Make sure your website gives them the answers they want. Make it easy for them to find the information they're looking for. Don't bury vital information in obscure places on your website – make it visible and give it high priority. If you don't know what questions your website visitors are likely to have, find out! Talk to your existing customers. Ask them about their biggest problems. Look on industry forums for the most common questions. Check out your competitors' websites.

151. Using too many fonts

Too many fonts will make your website design look amateurish and chaotic. Unfortunately, that will reflect on you and your business. Just use a couple of fonts that work well together throughout your website. That will give your website a unified, professional look.

152. Not having clear goals for your website

You need to have a purpose for your website. Once you have a goal, identify the specific markets you will target and then set measurable objectives to ensure you can measure their performance. Then track your website's performance.

153. Not placing contact information on every page

People need to know that the website they are looking at is owned and operated by a legitimate business and not a group of scammers. One way to demonstrate your company's trustworthiness is to provide your physical address and telephone number as well as your email contact details at the bottom of every webpage.

154. Not realising visitors aren't interested in you or your company

If you want your website to operate as an effective marketing tool, it must be completely customer-centric. That means everything from the content to the navigation on your website must be about your customers. It must answer their unspoken question, "What's in it for me?" They're not in the least bit interested in your company history, your company vision or mission statement. If they say they are, they're being polite or lying.

155. Using 'Welcome to our website' as your landing page headline

The bit of space for the headline on your landing pages is prime advertising space and its job is to grab the attention of every website visitor who lands on your website. It has mere seconds to hold the attention of that visitor so that they stay long enough for your website copy to work its selling magic on them. Using a bland headline such as 'Welcome to our website' is one of the deadliest website mistakes you can make. It's a complete turn-off for visitors and will get them hitting that back button faster than you can imagine.

156. Not having a blog

Writing blog posts is another way of engaging with people, and of encouraging visitors to stay on your site and return in the future.

Companies that blog get 55% more web traffic and 70% more leads than those who don't. And it's one of the best ways to reach your target audience with the sort of relevant, useful and interesting information they're looking for. A blog also helps your Google search rankings, since Google loves websites that provide fresh content and rewards them with higher rankings.

157. Not updating your blog

A blog's primary purpose is to give you a way to develop a relationship with your market. That's because people buy from those that they know, like and trust. When prospective and existing customers read your blog posts, they get to know you. You share information that they find relevant, useful and interesting. You might get so busy that you simply don't have the time to post regular updates on your blog. Unfortunately, the people who see your out-of-date blog won't know that. They will assume that either you don't have anything new to say (which means you're not keeping up with trends in the market or your company is not doing anything of interest) or that you can't be bothered (which they'll take to mean, you've lost interest in them). Either way, it reflects very badly on you and the company.

158. Not having a search feature

Users must be able to find what they're looking for and do so fast. Whilst this may not be imperative if your website or blog is a few pages long, it's an absolute necessity if your website or blog is large. This is particularly important if your website is an ecommerce site.

159. Not having sign-up boxes on every landing page

For best results, every landing page on your site (which is any page where *new* visitors are likely to enter it), should be focused on getting the visitor's contact details to begin your relationship with them. You should also remove as many unnecessary and extraneous links and buttons as you can without falling foul of the policies of the traffic sources you're using (such as Google AdWords, Bing Advertising, etc.).

160. Not offering free things to your website visitors

Offering website visitors free content is a must since it is a way of building a relationship with them and helping to convert them into paying clients.

What's more they are accustomed to receiving free products and services from websites like articles, case studies, white papers, ebooks, subscriptions to newsletters, and trials for software. They expect it. If you don't offer them something free, it makes your company appear tight-fisted.

161. Filling the homepage or other landing pages with large, irrelevant images

It's a big mistake to use a large image on your home or landing page, particularly if it has little to do with the page's main purpose. It means that there is less room for the information visitors actually want and expect to see. And if they can't see the information they want, they will leave your website.

162. Not having a 'Contact Us' page

You should have a dedicated 'Contact Us' page on your website that provides at least a couple of ways for website visitors to get in touch with you. It's normal to provide an email address that is monitored regularly and a contact telephone number. This is particularly important if you're asking people to make payments with a credit or debit card online – they need to know that should they have any questions or problems they can contact someone for assistance.

163. Hiding key information on the second screen of a web page

Many website visitors will never bother to scroll down to read or see anything beyond the first visible screen of any webpage which means if you've placed key information there, they won't ever see it.

Think of your web pages like the stories that appear in a newspaper: readers look at the headline to see if the page is of interest to them; they skim the page, looking for quick information like subheadings or bullet points that tell them what the page is about; and only then will they bother reading.

The top part of your page, like a newspaper story, must contain the most important information. That's because the majority of people

To apply for a free implementation session **worth £495** where we show you how everything in this book can be done for you, go to **completedigitalmarketingsystem.com/121**

63

will only ever look at or read the headline and perhaps the first few paragraphs. If you put the most important and relevant information at the end of your page there's a very strong possibility no one will see it.

164. Not having a Frequently Asked Questions page on your website

Visitors, particularly those who are still in the 'browsing' stage of the buying process, come to your website with questions.

The questions visitors have are barriers that stop them from taking any action on your website so unless you address them those visitors are likely to leave without even sharing their contact details with you. If you don't answer their questions and they leave, you will have lost the opportunity to foster an ongoing relationship with those visitors and convert them into paying clients at some point in the future. It also means you will have lost the opportunity to encourage those people to refer their contacts to you, which means more lost sales.

165. Not using compelling headlines

Compelling headlines grab the attention and interest of your website's visitors. Research has shown that headlines are the first things people look at to gauge whether or not to continue reading the page in front of them. They are mini advertisements. That's why you need to place unique, attention-grabbing headlines on each page of your website.

166. Not having a clearly defined purpose for your website

Your website must have one main purpose, and every page on your site must support that main purpose with its own. Moreover, every page must have *only* one purpose.

167. Having more than one call to action on a webpage

With rare exception, you should not have more than one call to action on any web page. The exceptions are when the two are closely related (such as a *standard* or a *deluxe* option, or where you can, for example, put a telephone number under an online form with text saying something like *"If your need is urgent or for fastest service call us now on [insert Freephone number...]"*.

168. Going wild with text and background colours

If you go crazy with colour combinations, there's a risk you make your website too hard to read. For readability, the best combination is black text on a white background. It provides contrast and yet doesn't cause eye strain. Black text on a neutral background like beige or light grey is nearly as good. Black text on a light colour background like light blue, light yellow or light green is okay. Avoid using reverse text (white text on a black background) except to emphasise short blocks of text. Don't use it on large blocks of text because it will strain the eyes of your readers.

Avoid weird text-background combinations like red text on a purple background.

You can check the contrast ratios on your website by using the free tool at AccessColor (**www.accesskeys.org**) which will analyse the colour contrast and brightness levels on your website.

169. Forgetting about offline prospects

Don't become an 'online myopic' who is so immersed in the online world that you forget about the offline world. Most people still live and work in the offline world and prefer physical things. Don't overlook the impact that actually holding a piece of paper or reading a newspaper can have on a prospective buyer.

170. Using faulty navigation

If a visitor lands on your website and has trouble navigating, he or she is just one mouse click away from a more inviting online destination. Good navigation on your website is a must if you want visitors to stick around long enough to be converted into customers

To apply for a free implementation session **worth £495** where we show you how everything in this book can be done for you, go to **completedigitalmarketingsystem.com/121**

65

171. Making users fill out the same information twice or more

Making your visitors fill out the same information again and again is almost guaranteed to make them feel incredibly annoyed, which is hardly the state you want them to be in before they buy or order something from you. The message they get is that you don't think enough of them to implement procedures that use already-provided information wherever you need it. Instead, you're expecting the users to do that for you. At the very least, ensure that your website doesn't lose data when a page refreshes or a user backs up. Don't force your users to go through multiple sites to place an order or book an appointment.

Wherever possible avoid making users login more than once. Your website should keep track of a user's login status in a way that is accessible to all parts of your website.

172. Asking for too much information too soon

Unless you're a loan company, you shouldn't expect your website visitors to willingly reveal lots of personal information to you, especially if you're only giving them a copy of your '10 Top Tips' or a free subscription to your blog. Don't demand they tell you their salary, marital status or shoe size. You'll scare them off. Leave asking for details other than their name and email address until they've had time to get to know you and your company.

173. Demanding information you don't need

Don't make people give you their company name if they're not buying your product or service for their company. Similarly, don't make all the data fields in a web form 'required' if the information is not really necessary.

174. Not giving the option to buy/order with a credit or debit card

You must make the buying process as smooth and easy as possible. That means giving people as many options to pay as possible like with a credit or debit card. Use a widely recognised online payment system.

To apply for a free implementation session **worth £495** where we show you how everything in this book can be done for you, go to **completedigitalmarketingsystem.com/121**

175. Not making it easy to navigate your website

You need to include consistent navigation elements on all your website pages. This is especially important for visitors who have arrived on a random page on your website via a hypertext link from somewhere else on the web.

The navigation elements on your web pages should let them know immediately what site they are on, where on the site they are and what the site has to offer them.

The navigation elements that should be present on all your website pages are:

- Homepage link

- Site identification

- Top level navigation links

- Site-wide navigation tools

- Contact information

176. Writing content that's all about you

When you write, avoid using words like "we" – write as if you are having a one on one conversation with the person you are speaking to. You will be going along the right lines if you use the word "you" a lot.

177. Using badly designed links

Links are the primary form of navigation on the web, which means your visitors should be able to identify and use the links on your website to move from one page to another or from one product image to another. The convention is to display textual links underlined and preferably in blue. Unfortunately, some websites ignore that convention and chaos ensues. Websites and web applications should make the clickability of onscreen components obvious at first glance, particularly for non-technical users. The very best way to ensure that

To apply for a free implementation session **worth £495** where we show you how everything in this book can be done for you, go to **completedigitalmarketingsystem.com/121**

67

your links look like links is to follow the convention: display textual links underlined and in blue.

178. Not changing the colour of visited links

Links are a key factor in navigation on your website. Visitors use them to move from one place to another. Knowing their past and present locations makes it easier for them to decide where to go next. They can exclude links that proved fruitless in their earlier visits. Conversely, they might revisit links they found helpful in the past. Most important, knowing which pages they've already visited frees users from unintentionally revisiting the same pages over and over again. They only get these benefits if they can tell the difference between the links they have and have not visited because the website shows them in different colours. When visited links don't change colour, people get confused and can unintentionally revisit the same pages repeatedly. As a result, they get frustrated with your website. And when they get frustrated, they leave.

179. Using tiny text

The problem with tiny text is that people with impaired vision can't read it. As people age, the minimum font size they can read increases. People over the age of 45 can be considered 'visually impaired' when it comes to reading small-print text. If they can't read it, it may as well not be there. That means, for many of your website visitors, your text is unreadable!

Perhaps worse is using tiny text on links, which people need to read in order to click on the link.

Most web browsers have controls for changing the size of text but they only work on sites that don't set font sizes. Some browsers allow users to override explicit font settings so that they can choose their preferred fonts and sizes. Unfortunately, in practice, most web users don't ever adjust or override the fonts in their browsers. They don't know how to do it. Instead of adjusting the fonts, most people simply avoid websites with tiny text. To avoid this, allow users to adjust the font size – don't set absolute font sizes. Don't use embedded text in images unless you know that anyone in your intended audience can read it. Don't use a font size smaller than 10 point.

180. Centring bullet points

Bullet points are supposed to mark items in a list but if they are centred (placed in the middle of the page), they are effectively neutralised. It forces readers to slow down to understand them and their eyes have to make laborious zigzag movements. Bulleted lists should be aligned to the left.

181. Not answering the question, "So what?"

Every claim that you make about your products or services triggers a question in your prospective customer's mind and that question is, "So what?" Claim that your new service is the work of a team of 30 experts and your customer will think, "So what? What does that mean to me? Why should I care?" That's why you should put all your copy through the "So what?" test. It will force you to think beyond the features of your products or services to come up with benefits. The benefits of your products or services are what will sell them to your customers.

182. Letting techies or graphic artist run your website.

Don't abdicate responsibility for your website to an HTML programmer or a graphic designer. That's because they will be more interested in the technical or visual aspects of your website, not whether it makes money for you. The focus of your website should be to make money for your business.

183. Not using the word 'FREE' on your website

People online love being offered free things. When they're offered free things that they consider worth having, they will happily give you their contact details in return. Building your database is one of the most important strategies in any business and your website is no different. So if you want to build your database, offer 'free' things to your website visitors. It will keep them at your site longer and it will increase the word of mouth advertising.

To apply for a free implementation session **worth £495** where we show you how everything in this book can be done for you, go to **completedigitalmarketingsystem.com/121**

69

184. Not giving visitors reasons to return

You need to give visitors a reason to stay on your website and then to return in the future. Giving them reasons to revisit your site will increase the likelihood that they will buy your products or book your services, or read more about you, or give you their contact details. One of the best things about a website is its ability to make people who are predisposed to purchase what you sell identify themselves. If you update your website often they will come back.

185. Using a busy pattern in your background

Busy patterns backgrounds are very distracting to the eye and tend to make it very difficult for visitors to read your content. Use solid colours, soft gradients, or subtly patterned backgrounds.

186. Using awful backgrounds

Many websites are nearly impossible to read because the text is superimposed over an awful background. Horrible backgrounds include those with overpowering colours, patterns, photographs and anything else that serves as a distraction.

187. Not asking for the sale

Poor marketing does not ask the client or customer to buy and does not give a time limit for the offer. You must ask your client or customer to purchase by a specific date and then give them step-by-step instructions on how to place the order. To get the customer to take immediate action, you must give him or her a time limit.

188. Using 'me too' marketing

'Me too' marketing is when you create a website that looks and reads like a replica of your competitors. Instead of showing why the business's products or services are unique and provide outstanding benefits, they repeat the same clichéd claims their competitors do.

So they say things like, "Best service", "Serving your needs for XX years", "Our customers are our biggest priority", etc. As a result, the website barely registers in the minds of visitors because it looks like every other website in the market.

For your website to generate a stream of high quality leads and stand out from the competition, it needs to be different and give proof that your products or services offer the best benefits to your customers. "Me too marketing" is when a business creates a marketing piece (advertisement, brochure, sales letter, website, etc.) that looks and reads like an exact copy of their competition's marketing. Instead of demonstrating why their product or service is unique and offers outstanding benefits, they say exactly what their competition says.

189. Using vague claims in your copy

Using claims like "Number One in the market" might make you feel good but it won't motivate people to buy your products or services. To do that, your sales message must promise prospective clients specific results. It should provide quantitative proof of why your product or service is better than the competition. You need to make your marketing promise so strong that people would have to be crazy to do business with any other company.

190. Focusing on the number of visitors your website gets

The number of visitors your site is not what matters. What really matters is how many of those visitors took the action you wanted them to take. For a commercial website only one thing matters: getting people to convert. That means they got to a page that said, "Sale successful" or "Contact details received, we'll be in touch soon". This is the action that translates into money. In web metrics terms, these are your 'target actions'. Assessing the total number of visitors to your site is only meaningful if you also know your conversion rate. The conversion rate is the percentage of visitors who engage in your target action.

191. Using Flash introductions

Flash introductions may look great but they ruin your SEO results, slow download times, and cause website visitors to leave without even waiting to see the rest of the website.

To apply for a free implementation session **worth £495** where we show you how everything in this book can be done for you, go to **completedigitalmarketingsystem.com/121**

71

192. Allowing too many advertisements on your webpages

Websites that feature a load of advertisements for other companies' products or services not only look tacky but also as if your company considers your visitors as a revenue stream with no other value. If that isn't bad enough, you also distract people's attention away from your website onto the advertised companies' websites.

When you're trying to make money from your website, it's very tempting to fit in more advertisements than you really should, or start using advertising formats that are in the way of the overall message. If a user can't find your content or message, he or she may click on the advertisement once, but won't return to your website again.

193. Not making usability a priority

Website visitors arrive because they want to find what they want and find it quickly. All too often, they're confronted with websites that designers have created to look "awesome" or worthy of a design award. They forget about how users can actually use their websites. To improve your website's usability, make sure your website:

- Loads fast because visitors are impatient and have short attention spans

- Contains content that is easy to find through good navigation

- Features content that's easy to read with subheadings and bullet points and surrounded by plenty of white space

- Has a search option so people can find exactly what they want

- Does not have pages that make visitors wonder what they should do

194. Putting too much on each webpage

An overcrowded webpage looks cluttered, messy and anything but attractive. That clutter can be anything from too many advertisements to too many category or website links. It looks desperate, as if you don't really understand your target market, so you're throwing everything at them in the hope something sticks. Less is definitely more.

195. Expecting visitors to scroll down to find relevant information

Many website home and landing pages feature a huge image that has little or no relevance to the page and which completely dominates the first screen. Visitors see very little text. That means they're left wondering what the point of the website is because the massive image tells them nothing about it. Their only option then is to scroll down to find out. Most will not do that. They will leave.

196. Using scrolling text and animations

Too much movement on a website is a horrible idea. It is bad for the eyes and bad for your message. Everything gets lost because visitors are too busy looking at the animations to see anything else. You must allow your visitors to actually read your content.

197. Offering jumbled layout and navigation

Visitors should be able to get to every page on your website within two clicks from any other page on your site. If they can't easily find what they're looking for they won't stick around to figure it out. Don't make it a struggle to find everything on your website. Word your links clearly. Use conventional names for standard links. Using 'clever' or 'cute' names for links will just annoy visitors and make it harder for them to find what they're looking for. Your content should be separated and given plenty of space. If it's cramped and the same size or colour it will be too difficult to read.

198. Using blocks of colours that are hard on the eyes

The colour palette you choose for your website is very important. Colours do affect people psychologically so you should choose a palette with that in mind. Avoid using large areas of bright colours like yellow, red, orange and bright pink because they tend to be hard on the eyes.

199. Using inconsistent designs for your webpages

It is vital that each of the inside pages are based on a similar design template and that they reflect your homepage. If your webpages don't look similar, you'll confuse your website visitors. They won't be sure if they're still on the same website if one page looks completely different to the next. If your design isn't consistent how can your message be?

200. Auto-playing music

Whilst auto-playing video is an extremely effective way of attracting attention, your website shouldn't automatically play music the moment a visitor lands. Because people can't always immediately tell where the music is coming from, they will more likely than not just leave your website.

Chapter 3
Remarketing

In a Nutshell

Generally, only 2% of shoppers convert on the first visit to an online store. Remarketing (or retargeting as it is also known) brings back the other 98%. So remarketing is a way of following up with visitors who didn't take any desired action (convert) the first time they visited your site.

You retarget those customers with banner ads that are relevant to the pages or products/services they viewed on your site. These ads will be shown on other websites that the potential customer visits.

Companies that leverage remarketing technology have seen as much as a 600% rise in response rates, according to James Mulvey and Dylan Touhey, co-authors of 'The One Guide to Remarketing'. [1]

Retargeting works by keeping track of people who visit your site and displaying your retargeting ads to them as they visit other sites online.

Essentially, remarketing involves placing a JavaScript tag in the footer of your website (on one page or many). This code creates a list of people who visit your site by placing anonymous retargeting cookies in their browser. This list allows Google (or one of the other retargeting vendors like AdRoll, Retargeter, Criteo, Ebay Enterprise (formerly Fetchback) or Tell Apart to display retargeting ads to your potential customers as they visit other sites.

---

[1] Mulvey, James; Touhey, Dylan, The One Guide to Remarketing, (One Net Marketing), 2012.

To apply for a free implementation session **worth £495** where we show you how everything in this book can be done for you, go to **completedigitalmarketingsystem.com/121**

75

Why is retargeting so effective?

Retargeting generates greater online sales by keeping your brand front and centre and bringing "window shoppers" back when they're ready to buy. Every time your customer sees your retargeting ads, your brand gains traction and more recognition. The high click-through rates (CTR) and increased conversions that are typical with retargeting campaigns underscore the value of good branding and repeated exposure.

By using remarketing, you can expect some enticing benefits:

- Reduced CPA (cost per acquisition) due to targeting a precise pool of prospects

- Increased brand awareness in a relatively short time period, without investing a large budget

- Increased conversions by remarketing to shopping cart abandonments

With this data, you can create display advertising that helps you to convert more of those lost visitors with a message or series of ads that 'speaks' to their stage in the buying process.

You can use remarketing to:

- Close visitors who left your website without taking any action

- Target users on the keywords or search terms they used to find your site

- Combine branding and direct response techniques to target users at different stages of the buying process

- Help to remind users about your brand as they research competitors

The following tips will help you to achieve your retargeting goals.

201. Use remarketing to re-engage

About 98% of your website visitors leave your site without completing a transaction. Since they visited, they're obviously interested. Retargeting can be as effective as search and is an essential part of the marketing mix. Best of all, it doesn't cost much.

202. There are different kinds of remarketing

There are quite a few different forms of remarketing. They include:

- Site retargeting

This allows you to show banner ads to anyone who has visited your website.

- Search retargeting.

This allows you to show banners to anyone that has visited your search engine and has searched for a phrase that you choose. For example, if you are selling financial services, then you can show banners to anyone who searches for the term 'financial services' and show them banners for your website's new financial services package. This means users don't even have to know about your business or have even visited your site for you to retarget them.

- CRM retargeting.

This allows you to show banners to people based upon nothing but their email address: you provide the retargeting network with the list of emails and you are free to show them banners. This is an expensive form of retargeting because to make it work effectively you will need a large email list to advertise to.

- Email retargeting

This allows you to show banners to anyone who has opened an HTML email field. You do this by placing your retargeting code inside the emails you send out. This allows you to greatly increase the audience and reach of your retargeting campaign.

- Audience retargeting

This allows you to remarket to a specific audience, which can be anything from women over 50 right down to people working in specific job positions.

203. Do customer research before you launch any campaign

You need to know this information so you can target your prospective clients effectively. Not doing this kind of research is the major reason remarketing campaigns fail.

Market research provides critical information and direction. It identifies needs and wants, motivation to buy and all the opportunities you can take advantage of with retarg

204. Set a goal for your campaign

Set a goal for your retargeting campaign. It might be something like:

- To boost traffic

If you don't have enough initial traffic going to your website right now then this may be the main objective of your retargeting campaign.

- To improve your conversion rates

You can use retargeting to improve all of your conversion rates (whether that's sign-ups, sales, requests for more information, etc.).

- To increase brand exposure

You can increase your brand exposure and become known as an authority in your market by focusing your retargeting campaign on branding.

205. Don't overlook your existing customers

Customers are often an overlooked segment for retargeting yet represent the highest possible return on investment (ROI) because you can divide them into their own retargeting campaign and show them banner ads specifically for other products you have that are related to the product they purchased from you.

206. Focus on specific audience segments

Focus on specific audience segments. For instance, if your objective is to improve your conversion rates, then focus on your visitors and engaged people. These are people who have come to your site but have not taken that next step so you can start showing them banners that reveal the benefits of buying your product or service (like bonuses, discounts or add-ons, etc.).

You can also focus on showing very specific banners to your prospects in order to increase the value of your product or service in their mind.

If you're interested in branding, then advertise to all these audience segments.

207. To create more relevant ads and offers, conduct customer research

Customer research will ensure you understand more about your target market, allowing you to create more relevant ads and offers that will really appeal to them.

208. Conduct no-cost psychographic research

To conduct no-cost psychographic research, use social media sites like Facebook and Twitter. Look at your customers' profiles to discover their likes, interests, and hobbies. Look for general patterns. Twitter will help you to find out what people within your target market are talking about and concerned with.

209. Discover how much to charge

Market research will tell you the size of your market and the demand for your product and service. You should be able to discover the number of people within that customer base who have a real need for your product or service, how much (if anything) they are spending to address that need today, and how much they spend in a year. You should be able to determine how much you can charge for your product or service from this kind of research.

210. Your competitors will reveal what techniques work in your market

Competitive analysis will ensure you understand what your competitors are offering and how your product or service offering compares. Begin by doing a Google search of your market. Look at all the organic Google results on page one and then the PPC ads: these represent your stiffest competition. Look at their landing pages, specifically their offers. What are they offering to your target market? What are the price points and what are the hooks they are using? Discovering the answers to these questions is a great way to find different ways of selling your product or service.

211. Look closely at your competitors' offers

Look at what products and services your competitors are offering. What are the pros and cons of the services that they are offering? What are the benefits that users get by purchasing their product? How do those benefits compare to the benefits they get by purchasing your product?

212. Let your competitors pay for your market research

Take a look at your competitors' sales pages to discover their sales process. If it's clearly working for them, take note of it because it's something they have obviously tested. If they're using long sales letters, do the same. Test the results. If you see they're only using an opt-in then using an autoresponder series to sell, try that too. Test the results.

213. Spy (legally) on your competition

Use SpyFu to look at the different PPC ads that your competitors are using. In particular, take note of the headlines they're using. If they've been using them for some time with good results, adapt their headlines for your retargeting campaign.

214. Know your cost per acquisition (CPA)

This is how much you are willing to pay to get one conversion, whether that's a sale or lead. To determine your CPA, you need to know how much profit you make per sale. If your product or service sells for £150 and it costs you £50 to deliver it, then your profit per sale is £100. The maximum CPA for you would be £100.

You also need to know your conversion rate for turning a lead into a sale. Let's say it's 5% so that for every 100 leads you make five sales. So if your product or service sells for £150 and you make £100 profit for every sale then five sales equals £500 profit. When you take that £500 profit and divide it by the number of leads (£500 divided by 100 leads) it equals £5 a lead. So your CPA is £5.

215. Define which niche market you will target with your campaign

The more specific your target market, the higher your ROI is likely to be since the banner ads and landing page you send them to will be more relevant: you won't be wasting ad impressions by showing them ads they're not interested in.

216. Test your frequency cap

This is an important tool that many don't think about. It's easy to set up and should be used and tested at various levels to see how often impressions should be served to each prospect. For some businesses, the frequency cap should be set very long (for example, you only serve an ad once every few days). For more impulse type buys, perhaps it makes sense to have a shorter frequency cap (for example, you show an ad six times per day).

217. Place your tracking code where it will increase your ROI

Frequently, you have a lot of website visitors that might not really be interested in buying. It's often easy to focus in on your target prospect list by honing in on pages that are visited by promising prospects. For example, if you have a sign-up funnel you could place the tracking code just within that funnel rather than site-wide. This dramatically limits your potential reach but can increase your ROI.

218. Use time of day targeting

You can target the time of day your impressions get served. If your customers typically buy on their lunch break or at night, set an appropriate time of day target.

To apply for a free implementation session **worth £495** where we show you how everything in this book can be done for you, go to **completedigitalmarketingsystem.com/121**

81

219. Use negative filters

Consider your entire visitor base and what might indicate that a visitor is not a likely candidate to buy. Don't ship your product to Europe or the US? Then filter out traffic from there.

220. Identify your best marketing content

Find what works before starting any retargeting campaign. The content must be effective on its own. That's because retargeting won't magically transform weak or poor content into wildly successful converting content. For maximum effect, you need to find where your conversions are already happening and focus your retargeting efforts there.

221. If you have a small budget, place your retargeting code on your shopping cart

This way you will retarget those people who abandoned their shopping carts. They will be the most specific and highly qualified visitors that you will target because if they placed something on a shopping cart but stopped short of buying it, they are very, very close to buying. It makes sense to show those people banners to encourage them to return.

222. If you have a large budget and a thin website, put your retargeting codes on every single page

Placing your retargeting code on every website page will allow you to retarget the highest number of people.

223. Find out where your competitors' banners are appearing

Using a free resource like www.tinyeye.com will allow you to find out where your competitors' banners are appearing online. (There are paid applications but if possible look for free resources that have excellent reviews, particularly when you're first dipping your toe into the remarketing water.)

From there, you'll be able to determine what your competitors are doing and what's working for them. You can monitor the success of their banner placements by how long they're kept on certain websites. Since your competitors are unlikely to continue paying for unprofitable website locations, you'll be able to find out which locations are profitable in your target market. You'll also be able to get inspiration from those banners for your own headlines and graphics.

224. Set a budget

Determine how much you want to allocate to spend on a test.

225. Have a strategy checklist

Create a strategy checklist. It should cover everything you need to do to create your strategy. It should include:

- Identifying your external audience

- Determining what sites you will capture your retargeting audience from. This will allow you to track how many conversions you get from the campaign.

- Deciding on a budget. If your budget stretches from £500-£1,000 a month, then you could put a retargeting code on every page of your website. If you have less to spend, choose a few pages or a section of your website to retarget. This will help to increase the relevancy of your ads and keep your budget low.

226. Build on your past successes

Once you know what works, you've got to make the most of that knowledge. Once your search retargeting campaign is up and running, determine which keywords are leading to conversions and then target users performing similar searches with look-alike targeting.

227. Make sure your banner features a strong call to action and sends users to a landing page

If your banner doesn't feature a strong call to action and doesn't send people to a landing page which makes the conversion process easy and simple, you'll just waste your campaign investment. Get the basics right before you launch!

To apply for a free implementation session **worth £495** where we show you how everything in this book can be done for you, go to **completedigitalmarketingsystem.com/121**

83

228. Don't retarget everyone

All site visitors are not created equal. To take a basic example, a visitor to the DVD page of a retailer's site is much more valuable than a visitor to that retailer's career page.

This practice of using data points to create a sophisticated picture of a site visitor is known as programmatic site retargeting (PSR). Other data points factored into PSR include pages viewed, referral data and shipping address, amongst others.

Marketers use this data to assign a "visitor score" to each user. The score, in turn, tells you how much you should bid to serve an impression.

PSR transforms site retargeting from an intelligent guess into a science, resulting in fewer wasted impressions, greater returns, and much better ROI.

229. Relevancy is key

Your retargeting campaign is only as strong as the data behind it. Use PSR **www.the-makegood.com/2013/05/23/the-power-of-tapping-into-all-your-data** to employ as much data as possible, from the referral sites and keywords that bring users to your site, to the sites that users travel to after leaving.

230. Don't stalk people

Set your frequency cap too high and your ads will haunt people, popping up whenever they click their mouse. The result of your retargeting campaign could then be a bitter backlash. Make sure you establish the right frequency cap to avoid annoying people.

231. Go with one site-retargeting vendor at a time

If you're using many retargeting vendors, they may end up bidding against one another in ad exchanges, thus driving up the price of your impressions. It's the equivalent of bidding against yourself at an auction. Even worse, keeping track of all that tracking code can turn into a big headache and put your data at risk.

232. Be methodical

Don't forget to place conversion and exclusion tracking code on your confirmation pages. After all, if someone just bought your product, it doesn't make much sense to continue to target them with display ads. You should be equally obsessive about your A/B testing. Just because two ads look alike doesn't mean they'll perform similarly.

233. Customise the ad experience for specific market segments

An IT specialist may not be interested in the same product features that would attract a C-level executive, so why use the same taglines to attract both groups? Collecting user demographic data enables you to segment your prospects by industry, job function and other criteria, so that you can create customised adverts to appeal to each audience segment.

234. Retarget your email marketing subscribers

You may have a large email database but the chances are that only around 20% of your subscribers are opening your emails. In order to draw their interest back to your business offering, use ad retargeting and bring these inactive leads back into your marketing funnel.

235. Maximise your social media reach

When sharing links on social media sites like Facebook and Twitter, you can take advantage of "smart" link shorteners that collect demographic data about the people who've clicked on your links. This will enable you to segment your social media visitors and create customised retargeting experiences for each group.

236. Use search retargeting to reach prospects who are actively searching for your target keywords

By creating specific retargeting-enabled landing pages for PPC campaigns, you can retarget prospects who have searched for specific terms with messaging related to those keywords. For instance, if a prospect has searched for a particular product that you sell, you can display ads for that product anywhere he or she travels on the web.

To apply for a free implementation session **worth £495** where we show you how everything in this book can be done for you, go to **completedigitalmarketingsystem.com/121**

85

237. Analyse your retargeting ROI by comparing retargeting conversions to a control group

By simultaneously running "reach" campaigns to attract new prospects alongside a retargeting campaign aimed at people who have already clicked your links, you can measure the impact of retargeting. Monitor how likely your retargeted prospects are to convert in contrast to the general population. This will help you keep track of the most effective forms of ad retargeting and how well it's working for your business.

238. Don't confuse retargeting with site retargeting

The most popular type of retargeting is site retargeting – the practice of serving targeted ads to users who have already visited your site, but there are six other types of retargeting:

1. Search
2. SEO
3. Email
4. Contextual
5. Engagement
6. Social

The most exciting of these is search retargeting, the practice of targeting users with display ads based on the keywords they entered into search engines.

239. Use product images in your banners and ads.

Product images will help to remind shoppers about the products they were interested in and were browsing before they left your site.

240. Keep your message clear

Make sure your creative message matches the landing page to which it is linked. That way the brand image / message you were originally communicating is carried throughout the conversion funnel.

241. Raise the stakes

Offer incentives with a sense of urgency. Test scarcity messages like 'Limited Time Only' or 'While Supplies Last', which prompt your customers to act quickly.

242. Use a call to action

Use phrases like "Learn more" or "Shop now". Offers perform better when a call to action is highlighted. For example, "Order today and receive free shipping!"

243. Test different pricing metrics

Are percentages or pounds more effective for your target audience? Even if the effective prices are the same, customers may respond differently to an offer for 10% off a £100 purchase versus £10 off a £100 purchase.

244. Don't be afraid to experiment

Try flash animation and rich media ads tied to a clear call to action to grab and hold your customer's attention. Test the results. If they work better than banners or ads without flash animation, use them in future campaigns.

245. Keep it brief

Say more with less. Keep your message succinct.

246. Don't ignore view-through conversions

Marketers rely on clicks as a key metric because they're easy to measure, but the vast majority of users never click on an ad – and most do it accidentally. Smart marketers look to other types of measurements, such as view-through attribution, which tracks users who convert after viewing display ads that they never clicked on.

This isn't to say that 100% view-through credit is the right measurement. It's not. Many marketers usually give view-through

To apply for a free implementation session **worth £495** where we show you how everything in this book can be done for you, go to **completedigitalmarketingsystem.com/121**

87

attribution a 65% allocation within a reasonable window of 14 days, which makes much more sense than the industry standard of 30 days.

247. Remarketing works best on high quality relevant traffic

Remarketing is the most effective when it's used on high quality relevant traffic. Analyse your visitors' behaviour. Look at factors such as the time spent on your website, where they came from (the traffic source), and their past purchase history.

248. Even if you're not doing pay per click you can use it

If for some strange reason you're not doing pay per click, you can just use an AdWords account for remarketing. It costs nothing to open and there's no minimum amount to spend. Test it with £10 if you want. You put a simple bit of code on your web pages, create a banner ad (or go to a site like www.elance.com or www.20dollarbanner.com to get banner ads designed) and the people who've been to your site will start seeing your ads everywhere they go online.

249. 49. Retargeting code works even when JavaScript is disabled

Retargeting can work even when people JavaScript is disabled by creating a transparent one-pixel image.

250. Retargeting code can be installed on any website

As long as you can input either HTML or JavaScript anywhere on a web page you can install a retargeting code. Typically the retargeting codes will be given an HTML format but if you need a JavaScript format then just ask the retargeting network.

251. If you have a WordPress website, you only need to install the code once

With WordPress, Joomla or Drupal you only really have to install the code once or in one place and it will automatically be shown on all of your website pages. This means that if you have a 599-page website with WordPress, Joomla or Drupal, all you need to do is install that code once and it will go on every single page, whereas with an HTML website you have to do each page individually.

252. Get more from your emailing lists with retargeting

Email retargeting is an easy-to-implement retargeting solution that lets you serve display ads to anyone who opens an email. Why use email retargeting?

- It allows you to create more opportunities to connect with your email subscribers

- It expands the reach of your email marketing campaigns

- It increases email ROI

253. Use retargeting on Facebook with Facebook Exchange

The Facebook Exchange is Facebook's real-time bidding platform. Real-time bidding is the technology that makes retargeting possible, and the Facebook Exchange makes it possible to serve retargeted ads on Facebook. It means when people leave your site, you can serve them display ads on Facebook.

That allows you to:

- Increase conversion rates with the power of retargeting

- Advertise on the world's most popular social network

How is it different than Facebook Marketplace Advertising? In comparison, Facebook Marketplace ads use Facebook-gathered data, such as location, gender, age, likes and interests, for targeting purposes.

Identify the segments you want to retarget. If you're already running retargeting campaigns, you know that segmentation is one of the best ways to get the right message in front of the right audience.

To apply for a free implementation session **worth £495** where we show you how everything in this book can be done for you, go to **completedigitalmarketingsystem.com/121**

89

254. Meet Facebook's creative requirements

Your retargeting image can be no larger than 100 pixels by 72 pixels. The title should be 25 characters long (including spaces). The body text should be 90 characters long (including spaces). No word used in the creative can be longer than 20 characters.

255. Rotate your Facebook ads

If you are consistently reaching a large majority of your audience, rotate your ads to keep potential customers engaged with your brand and products.

256. Be aware of cookie duration

Longer cookie durations expose the same ads to the same audience for an extended period of time and can quickly lead to creative fatigue. If you have longer cookie windows, cycle in fresh creative more often. Conversely, shorter cookie durations need less frequent creative refreshes as user list composition changes more quickly.

257. Use A/B testing

Rotating in different types of creative and testing them against each other ensures that you are receiving the best ROI from your ads. From the start, upload multiple versions of an ad to see which resonates with your potential customers the best.

258. Use a remarketing tag on YouTube

A remarketing tag can be used on all your web properties including social networks. If you have a large following on YouTube or Facebook it would be worth collecting data and testing out specific offers for your fans. Similarly, the tag can also be added to your external blog or to an e-newsletter. This approach is being used more often now the EU cookie law is in place.

259. Use Twitter for retargeting

While Google and Facebook have been offering the service for a while, Twitter's retargeting options are newer.

For the most part, Twitter's retargeting feature is straightforward and easy to use. A line of code is provided that is placed inside a website's backend, which drops an anonymous browser cookie that only stores site visit information. From there, when a bounced visitor logs into their Twitter account, the information is released and ads from that company can run while the user is logged into Twitter. It's a simple process that requires little to no extra work up front.

Unlike other retargeting or remarketing opportunities, Twitter's feature allows ads to run across mobile devices, tablets and so on. Because the user's information is saved within Twitter, it's not an abstract advertising system that reaches one customer a hundred times and not another customer. The potential reach is large and systematic, because the cookie storing your visit to an advertiser's site can be matched up to your account.

Twitter makes it simple for users to stop tracking, which makes it stand out from its competitors.

260. Create effective banners to successfully promote your site

Keep it simple: banner ads are displayed among a large amount of information and must often compete for the viewer's attention. Your customer may scan the page quickly, only laying eyes on your banner for mere seconds. Make those seconds count. An ad that is simple and to the point will get your message across in a short amount of time.

261. Keep your file size low

Web banners need to load quickly or they may not be seen. Make sure your file size is around 45-70kb so that it loads before your target audience has moved onto another web page and missed it.

To apply for a free implementation session **worth £495** where we show you how everything in this book can be done for you, go to **completedigitalmarketingsystem.com/121**

91

262. Always include a call to action

Getting visitors to click on your ad could be as simple as just telling them to do so. Using a simple call to action, such as "Click Here" or "Find Out More" reminds your viewer that there's more information or even a special offer available with a click of their mouse.

263. Build on your brand

Your web banner is a great way to build upon your brand's image. Make sure to design your banner using your corporate colours, fonts, and aesthetic – and always include your logo and tagline. Even if the user doesn't click through this time, they'll recognise your brand in the future.

264. Use proper placement

Make sure you place your banner ad on relevant websites, with customers that are already in the market for your product. You can be creative in your placement, advertising where your competitors aren't, but make sure you've got the right audience.

265. Recycle an old list

Recycle old lists for annual conversions. For example, a website that sells Father's Day presents can remarket to the same audience they built the year before. Similarly, you can recycle old lists for up-sell and cross-sell opportunities and multiple purchases. For example, if a user has bought a pair of running shoes, it would be worth targeting the same user with a campaign offering running gear or accessories.

266. Use all ad formats

Test different ad formats to discover which one gets the best results. You can use any of the following ad formats for a standard desktop and laptop campaign:

- 250 x 250 Squaresony

- 200 x 200 Small Square

- 468 x 60 Banner

- 728 x 90 Leaderboard

- 300 x 250 Inline Rectangle

- 336 x 280 Large Rectangle

- 120 x 600 Skyscraper

- 160 x 600 Wide Skyscraper

267. Keep your remarketing ads consistent with your website design

For a brand-building campaign, it's crucial that the design and logo of your ads are consistent with your website's colours and theme.

268. Feature the original product or service on your ad banner for conversions

If a user abandoned their shopping cart after looking at your £199 product or service, your banner ad should display the image of that £199 product or service.

Other ways to increase conversions include:

- Offer a discount

- Get users to subscribe to a newsletter

- Offer free shipping/delivery

- Offer a complimentary product

- Be relevant to the audience

- Have the same look and feel as your site

- Have a call to action

- Explain how you are better than your competition

- Show the user a photo of another product they previously viewed

269. Send users back to the original page you built your list from

Send users back to the same page they left previously (not the homepage). If you're up-selling users, send them to the new product or service you're promoting.

270. Create negative lists

The downside to remarketing is that it can be incredibly overwhelming, especially if you have bought a product but still receive advertising for it. One way to stop this is to create a negative audience to suppress previous AdWords buyers. If you create a list of users who do convert you can then add this list as a campaign-wide negative audience to ensure they don't receive offers for a product they have already purchased.

271. You don't have to confine remarketing to non-buyers.

You can put the code on your 'Thank You' pages that buyers see (or web pages that you only send paying customers to) and you can then serve up ads to customers – offering them additional products and services.

272. You can go beyond Google

If you've got a larger business with a lot of traffic, you will want to expand your reach. Once you're up and running on Google, you can go to some of the other ad networks to achieve this.

This is important because, whilst Google AdWords is a great place to start (particularly if your website isn't attracting much traffic) because it has no minimum monthly spend, you can only show banner ads on websites that are part of the Google Display Network.

Some of the other retargeting networks such as Retargeter, TellApart, Ebay Enterprise and Criteo have access to their own unique blend of dozens of networks with many publishers and often they have access to Google Display Network too. Criteo is one of the largest retargeting companies in the world but it has an extremely large minimum spend, as does TellApart.

Retargeter has a huge reach – about 99% of the ad inventory on the internet – so you know that you'll be able to reach your prospects wherever they are, but also charges a minimum rate for one campaign.

Meanwhile, Ebay Enterprise has some of the best reporting criteria so that you will know exactly what your retargeting ROI is. Once again, it charges a minimum spend for each campaign.

273. Choose placement targeting for locations where your ad can appear

You can choose to place your ad on an entire website, a section of a website (a selection of pages from the website) or a position on a single page.

274. If you want to place ads on pages related to your chosen topic, choose topic targeting

With topic targeting, you can place ads on pages that are directly related to your chosen topic. This is an alternative to selecting individual places where your ad can appear or individual keywords that will trigger your ad.

275. To get started with your remarketing list-making, you'll need to brainstorm

Create a list of all actions taken by users on your site. Determine which actions you should create unique ads for. Create remarketing lists that capture these individual groups separately. Create ads that speak to what makes them different.

276. Exclude people who did convert

Don't alienate your newest and most valuable customers by showing them more ads for the product they just bought.

You need to create a custom combination to exclude people who did convert. You may still want to show remarketing ads to these people, offering complementary products or inviting feedback. Still, they need to be on a separate remarketing list.

To apply for a free implementation session **worth £495** where we show you how everything in this book can be done for you, go to **completedigitalmarketingsystem.com/121**

95

277. Don't show the same ad to all your prospects

Be aware that your prospects will be at different stages of the buying cycle – some will only just be aware of your company name while others may have got as far as placing items in their shopping cart on your website before changing their minds. Prospects at different stages of the buying cycle will respond to different triggers.

278. Use audience targeting to show your ads to specific groups of people

With audience targeting your ads can be shown to specific groups of people as they visit Google Display Network websites.

279. Don't just create one ad

Try a combination of brand and lead capture ads. Use a variety of different banner ads instead of using a single ad over and over again.

280. Create a special landing page for your audience

Since remarketing involves targeting specific audiences, your normal landing page may not be suitable. Your remarketing landing pages need to create continuity between your campaign and the final push to action.

281. Create your remarketing lists carefully

When building remarketing lists consider the following things:

- What are you going to promote?

- What do your target users do on your site?

- Who needs a push to convert?

- Exclude anyone who did convert

- Use a profile in Google Analytics that excludes your internal IP address

282. Use the eight core elements of a good remarketing advert

When you're creating your remarketing ads, make sure they feature the eight core elements of a good ad. Those elements are:

- A strong call to action

- Brand colours

- Clear information

- Animation (where the platform allows for it)

- Tempting offers

- Relevancy to user

- Unique selling points (USPs)

- Eye catching images.

283. Discover why you're being shown certain ads

If you want to know more about why you are being shown certain ads across the internet (not limited to remarketing ads) you can use Google's Ad Preferences page to see how Google views you and to edit your advertising settings.

284. Don't waste your money on irrelevant ads

Only use ads that relate to the visitor's initial interest.

285. Display the ads subtly

Place your ads on the side of the web page rather than right in front of the visitor's face.

286. Use a campaign naming strategy from the outset

Before you start building remarketing lists, it is important to get a naming strategy in place as once you have created and named a list, this can't be changed in the future. If you are only creating a few lists, this will not cause you any problems but if you are looking to create multiple targeted lists, you will want to name them in a way that makes it clear to understand what the list contains for future use.

287. Exclude visits to your website from your internal IP

When creating a remarketing list in Google Analytics, the first thing you are asked is to select the profile that you want the remarketing list attributed to. If you don't have a profile set up in Google Analytics that excludes visits to your site from your internal IP, do this. You need to be able to see how much actual traffic your website generates from outside your organisation.

When it comes to building a remarketing list, there is no point following your employees round with adverts as they are never going to convert, only drive wasted impressions. Based on this, when you select the profile to allocate your remarketing list too, it is recommended that you select the profile which does not contain visits from your internal IP.

288. Place the remarketing code on your website now

The sooner you get the remarketing code on your website, the sooner you'll be able to start building your lists. Even if you don't want to start the campaign immediately, lists take time to grow so getting the code set up will give you a head start.

289. Build custom combination lists in Google AdWords

Custom combination lists are used by advertisers to de-dupe one list from another. For example, you may have two lists: one that contains all visitors who come into your site and another that contains all the people who have converted. You would use a custom combination list to target all visitors who have not yet converted on your website.

You can build these types of lists in Google Analytics but it's easier to create them using Google AdWords. Once they're running, it's also easy to see how many people you have in your list.

290. Get visitors back to your site using targeted ads

If you want to pull back visitors who have left your site, the easiest way to do this is by creating eye-catching adverts that are relevant to the visitor.

291. Create multiple campaigns for each desired goal

One of the mistakes people make when starting out with remarketing is to only create one campaign in Google AdWords that contains multiple ad groups. It's best to create multiple campaigns, with one campaign for each of your desired goals. This will not only give you a better understanding of what is working (and what is not) but also make managing the campaigns easier.

292. Your click through rate will be low but your conversion rate should be high

It's quite normal with remarketing and display campaigns for advertisers to get a very low CTR since ads are shown on websites where people aren't necessarily searching for a product or service. When people are searching on Google, they are actively looking for answers to questions or are looking to buy so the CTR is often much higher. So don't panic if your remarketing campaigns have a low CTR.

When you are looking at the conversions and conversion rate from your remarketing campaign, the number of conversions reported can sometimes look low. If this happens, switch on the column that shows you how many view-through conversions you have had as this gives you an accurate reflection of how many people have seen your ad before converting.

293. Send ads to dedicated and well-optimised landing pages

As with any PPC campaign, sending the traffic to the most relevant landing page on your site is going to help your conversions. Depending on how much traffic your campaign generates and how targeted the list is, it may also be worth considering creating dedicated landing pages to help boost the conversion rate further.

294. Keep refining the sites that show your ads

One of the benefits of remarketing with Google AdWords is that you can see the sites that your ads are being shown on. You can use this data to continuously refine where Google is placing your ads as you will find that some sites work much better than others.

To see this data, go to the 'Display Network' tab within your campaign in Google AdWords and then select the sub-tab for 'Placements'. You will then be able to expand on your 'Managed Placements' and 'Automatic Placements'.

If you haven't set up a Managed Placement campaign, Google will be determining which sites to show your ads on. You should use the Automatic Placement list to find sites that work well for you and add them into a Managed Placement campaign, but also find the sites that don't work for you and add them to your site exclusion list.

This will help in a number of ways:

- It will make managing your account much easier

- It will get you better results from your campaign

- It will limit the amount you're wasting since you'll be showing ads on sites that work hard for you

295. Not showing enough impressions can be almost as bad as showing too many

Not showing sufficient impressions to users can be almost as bad as showing them too many. The power of retargeting lies in its ability to keep your brand top of mind among users through continuous exposure. If you only serve a few ads throughout the month, it won't be enough to solidify brand awareness and brand recall. The optimal number is thought by many to be between 17-20 impressions per user per month, which is about one impression every other day. However, the perfect number of impressions will vary depending on YOUR market or industry sector so you need to test to find the perfect balance.

296. Test your remarketing ads

Test by changing calls-to-action, messages, photos, graphics, offers, landing pages, ad formats, and length of cookies. Don't change all of the variables at the same time. Instead, pick a few to test and keep notes of the changes you made in a document along with screenshots. While AdWords and Analytics can provide the raw numbers, it's up to you keep track of changes, hypotheses, formulas and conclusions, and to interpret the data.

297. Collect audiences

It's not necessary to have an active retargeting ad campaign to collect an audience from your website's traffic: you can use this website traffic to collect an audience who you can remarket to later. For example, you could create and collect an audience of people who only look at pages on your website that are about cat hats but do not make a purchase and remarket to this audience later when cat hats are on sale or when you get a new brand of cat hats. You know that at some point they were interested, so remind them about your products with an enticing offer. There are billions ways to segment and collect audiences, so keep your goal in mind and work backwards.

298. Check placement reports

Look at your remarketing reports to see where your ads are being placed on Google's Display Network. Check that ads aren't showing up on websites that don't compliment your brand or that have a super high bounce rate, and use negative placements to avoid showing up there again. Also review placement reports for websites that are converting well. If any really stand out, consider putting them in their own ad group.

299. Build a remarketing list from your YouTube account

You can build a remarketing list through YouTube for use within AdWords. That list can include viewers who have:

- Interacted with or viewed your YouTube videos

- Subscribed to, or unsubscribed from your channel

- Visited your channel

300. Be bold

With any online ad, you're competing with a multitude of other ads and distractions for a potential customer's attention. Whether they're on a website reading the news or scoping out a blog, your ad needs to be bold enough to catch their attention. Because of this, it's best to avoid white backgrounds which rarely stand out on a web page. Also, make sure to use large, bold typography to communicate your value proposition. In terms of imagery, pick strong, relevant images.

Chapter 4
AdWords

In a Nutshell

Using paid search via Google AdWords is an excellent way to drive traffic to your website. It can work many, many times faster than organic search (Search Engine Optimization or SEO) but it can be expensive if not handled correctly.

With AdWords (the brand name for Google's advertising platform), the trick is to manage campaigns to get the highest return on investment.

A poorly managed campaign can cost more than it brings in, but a well-managed campaign can keep your shop or company in business. It all comes down to how much you know about AdWords and how smartly you can manage your campaigns.

Essentially, success in AdWords is about getting in front of people who are looking for what you sell at this moment and getting them to respond. To do that, you need to really understand your audience and refine your message. And you need to keep testing and refining your message. The following tips will help you to create AdWords campaigns that generate sales and leads for your company.

301. Start by defining your AdWords goals

Have clear objectives for your AdWords campaign. Do you want to increase registrations by a certain percentage? Do you want to sell 100 products each week? Or to receive five phone inquiries each day from AdWords or display an ad 1,000 times for a certain price on a specific website? Advertisers can track multiple conversions in the same AdWords account. Once you know what you want, the next step is to track it and measure it.

302. Identify who your ideal customer is, so you can attract him (or her) to your business

Uncover the exact words people are using to shop for your services in Google. If you skip this step, or don't do it right, customers won't find you, and they'll go to your competitors instead.

Google provides a free tool (the Keyword Planner) to help you identify the most commonly-searched keywords. Most advertisers are aware of this tool and use it regularly to identify the keywords they want their ads to appear for.

303. Target your paid search

The more you target, the higher the return on investment will be on your paid search.

There are four ways to target using keywords (*also called "keyphrases"*):

- **Broad matches.** This is the most general form of targeting. With broad matches, search engines provide the broadest possible matches, including synonyms, plurals, and 'close matches' in any order and distribution. It means if users type in words or phrases that have just a hint of similarity to your chosen keywords, your ad could pop up. If your keyword phrase is 'red vintage dress', for example, users who search for 'vintage car with red interior', 'red antique book', 'black vintage dress' or 'vintage comics' might be shown your ad.

- **Exact matches.** With exact matches, the query must exactly match your keyword.

- **Phrase matches.** With phrase matches, your phrase must be included, but if the internet user puts in other words in addition to the phrase match your ad will still appear.

- **Negative keywords.** Negative keywords are words that, when included in the user's query, will not cause the search engine to list your ad, even if other keywords in the query match.

304. Track your success

One of the simplest ways to track success is a feature in AdWords called conversion tracking. It shows whether a click on an ad resulted in a desirable behaviour on the website. It places a cookie on the searcher's computer after a click on an ad. This cookie expires in 30 days.

If at any point during that 30-day period a conversion page is reached on that computer, it is recorded in AdWords. The conversion is credited to the keyword that triggered the ad, on the date of the click.

305. Group keywords correctly

With AdWords, you can create campaigns and ad groups to manage different types of campaigns. For example, if you have a product campaign and a content campaign, each of them can be managed separately. Within each campaign, you can break down your ads and keywords into ad groups.

Not using multiple ad groups is one of the biggest mistakes people make. Instead of segmenting their ads into groups based around similar types of keywords, they lump all of their keywords into one ad group and show everyone the same ad.

The problem with this approach is that the ad being shown should match the keyword being searched. The closer the ad copy matches the keyword, the more likely people are to click on the ad (and eventually order).

If you don't break up your keywords into different ad groups, then you'll lump everything together underneath one ad copy. This doesn't allow you to customise the ad to be a good fit for the term being searched for. The more you break up your ads and keywords into themes, the easier your campaigns will be to monitor and optimise.

To apply for a free implementation session **worth £495** where we show you how everything in this book can be done for you, go to **completedigitalmarketingsystem.com/121**

105

306. Use the right keyword matches

AdWords allows you to add keywords to a campaign in one of three ways: broad match, phrase match or exact match.

A broad match keyword means that your ads will show if the keywords are used in the search, regardless of the word order.

A phrase match keyword means the keyword phrase needs to show up in the search as a complete phrase in the order you enter it.

An exact match keyword works just like it sounds. The term being searched needs to exactly match the keyword that you entered in AdWords.

The type of match you use will have a big impact on your ads. A broad match will deliver more impressions, but it will be more imprecise since it will show up for terms that aren't a tight fit for your products or the ad.

On the flip side, phrase and exact matches often provide a higher conversion rate, but they can deliver significantly fewer impressions, which means you may not reach as many people as you need to.

In some niches, the number of people looking for what you're selling is low, so if you limit too much with exact matches, then you're not going to get very much traffic. On the other hand, if you have too many broad match terms, then you may not get a high enough ROI on your ad campaign. The best scenario is to tweak your matches to find what works best for your business.

Start with exact matches and then expand to phrase and broad as needed. If you aren't getting enough impressions and conversions with exact matches, then you can add the terms as a phrase match and eventually as a broad match. On the flip side, if you aren't getting good results with a broad match, you can scale back to use only exact and/or phrase matches.

307. Uncover which keywords your competitors are bidding on

There are several tools available to help you perform this research and it's worth researching to find those with the best customer reviews. If you find several competitors bidding on the same keywords, there's a good chance that those are worth bidding on (otherwise your competitors wouldn't continue to invest in them).

308. Prioritise your keywords

Decide which keywords have the highest chances of being profitable right from the start, based on their relevance, competitiveness and cost. Those are the keywords you want to start your initial testing with.

309. Do use negative keywords

AdWords allows you to use negative keywords as a way to exclude keywords that are not a good match for your product.

For example, if you own an e-retail store that sells designer women's shoes but not running shoes, then you won't want your ads to show up on searches for "women's running shoes" but do want them to show up on searches for "women's shoes." Thus, you can add "running" as a negative keyword, and your ads won't be shown for any searches that include the word "running."

Negative keywords can be added at both the campaign and the ad group level. Thus, if a word should be excluded from only one particular ad group, then you can exclude it at the group level, but if you want it excluded from the entire campaign, then you can do that as well.

310. Find negative keywords in Google Analytics

To find words that should be excluded from your ads, you need to delve into Google Analytics since it has more detailed information than AdWords about specific keyword searches. Within Analytics, click on "Acquisition," then "AdWords", and then "Matched Search Queries." Next, click on "Query Match Type" and then either "broad match" or "phrase match" to view the exact keyword phrases people are searching for and which ones aren't converting well. Once you find phrases that aren't converting, take a look to see if a negative keyword can be added to eliminate that keyword from your campaign without excluding terms that are performing well.

311. Don't fall in love with your ad copy

Crafting the copy for an ad takes a lot of research and creative effort. It's all too easy to fall in love with the resulting ad. That's a mistake if the numbers show that it's not working.

You should always be testing your copy. Try two different headline variations, the same headlines but different body copy, or the same copy but a different call to action. Testing different variations will help you to know what works best. Sometimes mentioning a benefit will increase click-throughs and/or conversions. Other times, a different headline will improve your results. You'll never know until you test.

Once you do start testing, resist the temptation to fall in love with subsequent ads! Once you have between 20 to 40 clicks, choose the one that's getting the best results, which means the highest click-through rate, the highest conversion rate, or the lowest cost per acquisition (CPA), depending on what makes the most sense for your business. Don't make the mistake of loving your clever copy more than the results you're getting.

Once you have a winner for one test, turn off the loser, and change the ad copy again. Always try to beat the winner until you're happy with the results. You may be surprised that this kind of testing can eventually lead to doubling your conversion rates and halving your cost per acquisition.

312. Do bid on your own brand

Many business owners make the mistake of not bidding on their own brand. They assume that since they already rank for their own brand, they don't need to advertise for it.

But if they're not advertising their brand, other companies will. They'll use that company's brand name for an ad group and target their visitors. Yes, the company may rank first for the organic term, but their competitor may be advertising directly above that result.

In many cases, it makes sense to bid the highest for your own brand since people who are searching for your company are the most likely to convert. You want to make sure you're at the very top for your own brand name, which means you can spend the most on branded terms.

313. Know the lifetime value of your customers

Before you spend anything on AdWords, you must know the lifetime value (LTV) of your customers. LTV is the projected revenue that a customer will generate during their lifetime.

If you don't know your customers' LTV, the basic formula is:

(Average Order Value) x (Number of Repeat Sales) x (Average Retention Time). Kissmetrics.com has an infographic that shows the LTV of a Starbucks customer. It explains why Starbucks offers free Wi-Fi and comfortable couches: it's not focusing on selling a cup of coffee but on retaining a customer potentially worth over £14,000.

Let's say your customer LTV is £1,000. This means that you'll earn £1,000 on average over the lifetime of doing business with your customer. If you're paying £60 per acquisition, then you're okay, because you're making more per customer than you're spending. But if your LTV is £40 rather than £1,000 and you're spending £60 per acquisition, you'll go out of business before too long.

A lot of companies don't know their LTV so they don't know what a good CPA is.

Let's say your customers stay with you an average of six months and pay £30 per month, then your LTV is £180. In this scenario, you'll be doing okay even if your Google CPA is £100. It all depends on what you're selling and what the LTV is for your business.

You may lose money at the beginning to acquire a new customer, but make it back over the lifetime of doing business with that customer.

314. Get your ads in prime position

You absolutely have to aim for your ads to appear on the left hand side. On average, ads on the left get at least 10 times as many clicks as ads on the right, so you want to make sure that you are in one of the top three positions.

315. Know who you're competing against

You need to know who you're competing against, what keywords they're using, and what their landing pages look like.

Specifically, you want to put yourself in your customers' shoes and see which ad you're most likely to click on. Then, once you do click (although it's recommended to find ways to do it without actually clicking on your competitors' ads and making them pay for it), pay attention to their landing pages, and compare theirs with yours.

Which one is the most appealing? Which one would you rather go to if you were the customer? Take some notes and work out what you can improve on your landing pages. Do you need a better design, a cleaner look and feel, security factors, testimonials, social proof, authority or something else? Create a checklist based on the things you find.

Begin by scanning your competitors' ad copy to see what you can learn and apply. Then, scan their landing pages to see how you can improve your pages. Once that's done, test new ad copy based on what you've learned, then create new landing pages and test them against your old ones. Keep testing until you improve your conversion rates.

316. A small AdWords budget may be an exercise in frustration rather than success

If your budget is too small, you won't have enough to test your ads until they start performing well. It takes time to run and optimise your campaign to improve your ROI. A small budget also means you're going to burn through your campaign and will have to wait until more money is available. That gets frustrating.

That's why **it's better to** start with a large enough budget that allows you to drive a significant amount of traffic and gives you time to tweak and optimise your campaigns. Make sure you also stick with the campaigns long enough to give them time to gain traction and to give yourself time to figure out how AdWords works and how you can get the highest ROI.

317. Send ecommerce visitors to the right product or category page

Make sure you send ecommerce visitors to an appropriate product or category page not your homepage

It's better to send people to a landing page or a product or category page where they will see a direct match to the ad they clicked.

Make sure the page people land on matches the ad copy they clicked.

318. Understand how bidding works

Cost per click bidding (CPC) is also referred to as pay per click (PPC). It's a pricing model where the advertiser pays only for clicks on an ad. The ad can display 500,000 times, but if no one clicks, it does not cost the advertiser. Naturally it's in Google's best interests to show ads that receive clicks: keywords with higher CTR are rewarded with better quality scores.

319. Specify a bid limit for automatic bidding

Automatic bidding allows AdWords to manage your bids. This model tries to generate the most clicks possible within the budget. By default, the system automatically chooses whatever bids it determines will earn the most clicks.

The automatic bidding model finds clicks, nothing more. It does not help achieve higher conversions, profitable ad positions or better click costs. If you use this model, check the box labelled "CPC bid limit" and enter an amount. Otherwise, you may pay far more for a click than makes sense for your business. The bid limit applies to all ad groups in the campaign and prevents AdWords from showing ads in ultra-competitive, overly expensive auctions.

320. Consider automatic bidding to start with

If you are brand new and have no idea what price range to bid on keywords, using automatic bidding for a short period of time can help you learn what clicks cost. You can then switch to manual bidding with that data.

321. Improve your campaign's conversion performance by enabling enhanced CPC bidding

To use enhanced CPC bidding, you must have conversion tracking set up in the account. The feature does not require a minimum number of conversions, so you can turn it on immediately.

If the campaign does not have any recorded conversions, enhanced CPC has no effect on the bids. But, once conversions start recording, enhanced CPC can use the data to raise or lower bids if a conversion is more or less likely.

Enhanced CPC can raise a bid as much as 30% if a conversion is likely. If AdWords data shows a conversion is less likely, it can reduce the bid with no bottom limit. The campaign's daily budget still applies, so overall costs do not increase.

322. Understand CPM bidding works on a pay per impression model

Advertisers specify a maximum price they are willing to pay for every 1,000 times an ad is displayed, whether it is clicked on or not. A click on an ad does not incur an additional cost to the advertiser.

CPM bidding is available for the Google Display Network only. If Search is selected in the campaign's settings, the CPM option does not appear as a bidding option.

323. How to decide what to bid

If you are not sure how much to bid on a keyword or how much you can spend per day on the selected keywords, use the Traffic Estimator tool found in the Reporting and Tools tab. This tool helps forecast a keyword's price range, level of competition and daily search volume. The data can also help you decide on a budget for the campaign.

It does not guarantee a particular cost per click or traffic volume, but it can provide some sense of the keyword's potential.

To use the tool, enter the proposed keyword or a set of keywords, a Max CPC, and a daily budget. The tool shows you, keyword by keyword, the average estimated CPC, the total number of estimated clicks and the total estimated cost per day. Global monthly searches shows the approximate 12-month average of search queries for the keyword on Google Search, specific to the match type entered.

324. Don't let a fear of click fraud stop you using Google AdWords

Imagine you've set a budget of $100/day and you're bidding $4 per click then one of your competitors clicks on your ad 25 times. Your daily budget is blown and you have no customers. This is known as 'click fraud'.

The fear of click fraud is enough to put many business owners off ever using AdWords, which is a great pity. Yes, competitors can still click on your ads, but Google will detect this and you will not pay for these fraudulent clicks.

Google has sophisticated tools to identify which clicks are fraudulent and which are real. It analyses each click, considering various data points like IP address, the time of the click, duplicate clicks and click patterns, then uses this data to try to isolate and filter potentially fraudulent clicks before they appear in account reports. Google filters and discards suspicious activity, like repetitive clicks, as well as clicks and impressions from known sources of "invalid activity."

You'll still see "invalid" clicks which are clicks Google determined were fraudulent – but you won't have to pay for those clicks.

Don't let concerns about click fraud stop you from using AdWords to grow your business.

325. Your ad text is critically important

A web user is looking for an answer to a question, a solution to a problem, or a way to fulfil a need or desire. If you've got what the searcher needs, the ad text is your opportunity to convince him to visit your website. Unfortunately, the amount of text you can squeeze into the ad is extremely limited: you have a 130-character limit (including the Display URL).

326. Your ad will face stiff competition for your prospect's attention

Your ad will not only be competing against other AdWords advertisers, but also against organic and sometimes local business (Google Places) results. On a crowded search results page with many options, your ad needs to set you apart and convince the searcher that your website has what he or she is searching for.

327. There are only five lines in an AdWords ad

AdWords text ads include four distinct lines plus a line with the Destination URL:

- The first line is the headline or title of the ad. It allows up to 25 characters, including spaces

- The next two lines, called Description Line 1 and Description Line 2, allow up to 35 characters each, including spaces

- The fourth line, called the Display URL, allows up to 35 characters

There is one additional field to complete, the Destination URL. This specifies where a click on the ad "lands" on the website: sometimes this page is called the landing page.

328. Your ad must meet strict formatting and style rules

Your ad must meet AdWords strict guidelines. They are:

- You cannot skip lines. All five lines of your ad text must have a value

- Ads must be written with proper spacing. Your ad may not be approved if you omit spaces or add extra spaces or characters between words

- Punctuation and symbols must be used properly in a sentence in the ads, not as a way to attract attention or replace words

- AdWords does not allow repeated punctuation and it limits exclamation points to one per ad (and only in the description lines, not in the headline or Display URL)

- "Texting" language is not allowed

- AdWords does not allow ad text with unnecessary repetition

- Ads must use proper capitalisation. You cannot write an ad with all uppercase letters (although all lowercase may pass). You are allowed to capitalise the first letter of each word, if you wish

- •The Display URL is subject to additional rules. AdWords does not display *http://* or *https://* in ad text, so these characters do not count toward the 35 character limit. The *www.* Is optional: if you choose to include it, the four characters do count toward the character limit. If the Display URL is longer than 35 characters, it will be truncated

- The Display URL must be a website and the Destination URL must be an HTML page. It doesn't matter what the file extension is (*.htm*, *.html*, *.asp*, *.php*, *.jsp*: any will do)

- You cannot display or link to an email address or a non-HTML file (PDF, MS Word, JPG, etc.)

- The domain of the Display URL must match the domain of the landing page URL

- You are permitted to use a redirect, like a URL shortener, as long as the final destination domain matches the displayed domain. In other words, if you advertise a website, you must send visitors there, not to a different site

329. Your ad must follow AdWords' editorial policies

Ads are subject to an extensive list of editorial guidelines. If an ad violates a policy, it is labelled "disapproved" and cannot be displayed. Once you correct the issue and resubmit the ad, it is eligible to participate. However, if Google determines that a violation is an extreme policy breach, or if your ads are repeatedly disapproved, Google can suspend your account or ban you from AdWords.

So your ad must meet the following guidelines:

* Don't mislead people
AdWords requires ad text to accurately represent the content on the landing page. If the landing page promotes something different, the ad may be disapproved. The policy requires that ads and landing pages display real, accurate information about the advertiser.

* Be polite
Don't swear or self-censor in ad text.

* Support competitive claims
Don't say you're better than a competitor unless your landing page clearly explains why.

* Support superlative claims
If you use a superlative claim in your ad, a credible third party must be cited on your landing page.

* Avoid generic calls to action
AdWords does not allow calls to action that could apply to any ad, regardless of content. For example, generic phrases like "click here", "visit the website" and "select this ad" don't pass. Examples of acceptable ad verbiage include "buy now", "order today", "learn more", "browse our catalogue", etc.

* You can use phone numbers
You can display a phone number in your ad, with two exceptions: not in the Headline or in a Sitelinks extension.

* Some topics are limited or off-limits
AdWords restricts some topics, including abortion, sexual services,

alcohol, casinos and gambling, drugs and drug paraphernalia, endangered species, counterfeit documents, fireworks, hacking, health care and medicines, illegal products and services, solicitation of funds, tobacco products, trade sanctions and restricted parties, traffic devices, underage and non-consensual sexual acts, and weapons.

- Prices, discounts and offers must be found within two clicks of the landing page

If an ad promotes a price, discount or offer, it must be found within two clicks of the landing page. For free offers, you're not required to explicitly say "free", but it should be obvious to the site visitor.

If you use the words "guarantee" or "warranty" in your ad, AdWords requires that you provide the details and any major limitations.

- Pleas for popularity are now allowed

Your ads can't encourage searchers to click on the Google +1 button.

- Personal information must be held securely

Advertisers must use secure servers when collecting personal or financial information. In addition, advertisers must clearly disclose when they do this and request permission from visitors. Sites collecting payment or financial information must disclose prices and billing practices in an easy-to-understand way. Permission must be obtained before processing payments.

- Arbitrage is not allowed

Advertisers cannot advertise websites designed to persuade visitors to click on more ads.

330. Make your ads clear and simple

Effective ads are clear, simple, and relevant. You have a very small amount of space, 130 characters (including the Display URL), to convince a searcher to click on your ad and learn more. With so many other websites vying for the searcher's attention, how can you help your ad stand out in a crowd?

Make it relevant. The ads you write should closely reflect the theme of the keywords or placements in the ad group. AdWords does not usually work well when generic ads are displayed for specific searches. If you can present the searcher's query (or something close to it) in the text of the ad, you have a greater chance of winning the click.

331. Use both benefits and features in your ad

When you write an ad, use both benefits and features. What's the difference? Benefits tug at the searcher's heartstrings, convincing him or her that it provides the solution to a problem, fulfils a need or delivers success.

Strong ads often open with benefits to connect with the searcher and convince him or her to learn more.

Features describe the 'nuts and bolts' aspects of the offer, which might be free shipping or a gift. Use features to help close the decision process for the searcher, to convince him or her to use your company.

332. Test different layouts

AdWords does not allow excessive capitalisation in ad text, but it does allow ads to be rendered with uppercase and lowercase letters. So test a version of an ad with every word starting with a capital letter and then another with only sentence case. Find which results in a higher click-through rate (and conversion rate, once conversion tracking is set up).

Other elements to test include:

* The use of numbers

* The use of prices

This technique can work if the searcher is truly cost-conscious and your prices are lower than competitors.

333. Consider using dynamic keyword insertion

Dynamic keyword insertion (DKI), sometimes referred to as "wild card", is an ad text trick that can make an ad seem more relevant to a search query by inserting the keyword into the ad text. With DKI, you place a piece of code in the ad text. This tag can be placed in any or all lines. When someone searches Google for one of the keywords in your ad group, the tag is replaced by the keyword that triggered the ad.

334. Be careful when creating keyword lists using DKI.

You must be sure that the rendered text reads well and makes sense.

335. Use ad extensions to help your ads stand out

Extensions are "add-ons" that make ads appear more relevant or useful for a searcher. They can also occupy a larger area on the search results page. There is no additional cost for using extensions, but if the extension connects a searcher with the advertiser, the advertiser is charged. You can use multiple extensions for each campaign, but not all will be are applicable for every situation. There are four types of extensions: location, sitelinks, products and call.

* Location extensions
A location extension improves a text ad by displaying the business address beneath, as well as a link to directions from Google Maps.

Location extensions are extremely helpful for local businesses with brick and mortar offices or stores. If you operate a web-based business or if customers do not visit your location, you will not use this extension.

* Product extensions
These allow advertisers with ecommerce websites to display product images with AdWords ads.

Product extensions appear as a set of thumbnail images below the ad text, including the title and price of the product.

As with most extensions, the price for a click on a product thumbnail corresponds to a click on the text ad.

* Sitelinks
Sitelinks are one of the simplest ways every advertiser can improve ads. A standard text ad offers a single landing page option, associated

with the headline and the display URL. Sitelinks allow advertisers to display up to six additional display URLs below the ad, to connect searchers to the most interesting pages or sections of the website.

Sitelinks can drive special promotions, reinforce conversion incentives and promote additional areas of the website.

They are displayed for top-ranked ads only. Each sitelink includes a display URL (up to 35 characters) and a destination URL (up to 1,024 characters).

• Call extensions
These allow advertisers to associate a trackable phone number with text ads. Call-only applies to ads on mobile devices using CPC bidding. With this extension, the destination URL is replaced by a clickable phone number. Instead of sending visitors to a website, a click triggers a phone call to a number specified by the advertiser.

336. When you test ideas, fail fast

If you test an ad and it fails, move on quickly. Once you get the results, cut your losses and try something else.

337. If you test an idea and get a lukewarm response, tweak it

If your ad idea gets an okay but not overwhelmingly positive response, play with it. Change the title, the price or the offer. Seek feedback and try again. If the changes still get a mediocre response, move on to something else. Don't waste any more time or money on that idea.

338. Don't ignore video

AdWords offers several video ad formats, including "click-to-play", in-stream video, in-video static image ads, amongst others.

Click-to-play videos are initiated by the website visitor. People who see the ad must click to view a video. If the viewer clicks a second time or on the Display URL, he or she is taken to the ad's destination URL. Pricing depends on the model selected by the advertiser, CPC or CPM.

With CPC, advertisers do not pay when someone plays the video: the charge occurs when the viewer clicks through to the destination URL.

With CPC bidding, click-through rate is an important factor in the auction, so ads with low CTR may have a difficult time winning placements.

With CPM bidding, advertisers pay for every 1,000 impressions the ad's opening image receives. With this pricing model, CTR is not as important because clicks are not part of the equation.

339. Weave keywords into your ads

Try to work your keywords into your ads as seamlessly as possible in both your headlines and body copy. An Overture study conducted by AC Nielsen stated *"Users were nearly 50 percent more likely to click on listings in which the keyword was included in both the title and description."*

340. Make sure your keywords are the words your customers use

Customers search using terms and phrases familiar to them, not your business lingo.

341. Generic keywords will empty your pockets

Choosing a generic keyword will boost your traffic but may not bring in sales. Keeping your keywords specific and targeted will reduce charges for unneeded click-throughs.

342. Get inside the mind of your potential customer

When a potential customers has a problem that your product or service can solve, you need to know what words they use to search Google for a solution. Make a list of these words.

343. Research your prospects' search terms

Go to Google and search those terms your prospects use when they're looking for a solution to their problem. What comes up? Who's advertising? If there are fewer than eight AdWords ads on the right side, then you can get in for a minimum of five cents – that's how much the eighth position costs. There might be dozens of bidders, showing up on the second, third and fourth pages of results, and the top positions will usually be several dollars a click.

If, however, you do all the cool stuff, increase your CTR and have sitelinks, etc. it's not unusual to pay under a dollar in a category where your competition are paying several dollars.

344. No advertisers is not a good sign

If there are no advertisers, either it's an undiscovered market (not likely) or people searching for that term tend to not spend much money.

345. Lots of advertisers means competition will be stiff

If there are LOTS of advertisers, it's a big market with lots of competitors. *You have the most latitude when the situation is halfway in between:* two to eight other bidders is a nice number, because if that's the situation with "obvious" words then there are undoubtedly a lot of bargain keywords too.

346. Create a large list of keywords

Perry Marshall, AdWords Expert, says you should compile a list of 100 words and phrases. A list of 200-300 keywords is better. Divide your keywords up into clusters of 5 to 25 closely related terms. You're going to assign a different ad to each of these tight groups.

347. You need to choose words for your ad with exceptional care

You don't have many words to play with on your ads: you get 25 characters on the first line, 35 characters on the second and third lines, and a space for your URL. That's why you need to spend time picking the ones you use.

348. Use Google's Traffic Estimator

Google's Traffic Estimator tells you how much traffic to expect and how much it will cost. Set your daily budget. If you can afford it, err on the high side, which will make testing go faster. The traffic estimator will give you an idea of how fast your campaigns will develop.

349. Write a second ad for every campaign

Above each ad in your AdWords campaign is a link that says 'Create New Ad'. Click on it and create a second ad for each campaign. Make it different from your first ad. Vary the words, the capitalisation, verbs, concepts, etc. Google will evenly split the traffic between the two ads and you can directly compare them.

350. Don't avoid ultra-competitive markets

Don't avoid markets simply because they seem awash with competitors. There's nothing wrong with going into a fiercely competitive market, according to AdWords expert Perry Marshall. "The more competitors there are, the more money is available to the winners," he says in the "Ultimate Guide to Google AdWords". You can win in almost any market provided you test your ads, use persuasive descriptions of your products, use email to follow up and watch your numbers, he adds. It's important to realise however that the more bidders there are, the more money you'll have to invest in testing before you'll become profitable.

351. Monitor the two ads and delete the weaker one

After your ads have got 25 or more clicks, you should be able to see a clear difference between the two. Delete the one that has the lower CTR and write a new one. By improving your ad, you will get more traffic without spending any more money.

352. Analyse the performance of your keywords

Look at how the keywords in your ad campaigns are performing: some will be performing well and others not so well. Take the ones that have been performing unusually compared with the others – those that are much cheaper or more expensive, or which get much higher or lower CTRs than others. Delete them from the existing ads and stick them in their own new campaign. Write two new ads using those keywords and monitor how they perform against your original ads.

353. Keep brainstorming new keywords

As your ad campaigns progress, you will think of or discover new keywords. Test them.

354. Track the conversions of each AdWords group

You will find that some of your keywords convert to sales while others don't. Stop bidding on the non-converting keywords to save yourself money.

355. Write concise sentences

Use your keywords in clear, concise sentences – with proper punctuation, capitalisation, spelling, grammar and spacing.

356. Your ad must speak directly to your prospect

What would appeal to you if you were a customer? What do your prospects need to read to get them to click on your ad and visit your site?

357. See what your competition is doing

Check out what's working for your competitors. Think of a way to write their ads even better.

358. Grab your prospects' attention with your headline

Your headline is the most important part of your ad. Take the time to come up with a hook that will grab your prospects' attention.

359. Emphasise a benefit

State the most compelling benefit of your product or service. If your USP is that you have the widest variety, highest quality, best customer service or lowest price, mention it.

360. Make your offer unique

For maximum impact, make sure what you offer is different and sets you apart from your online competition.

361. Ask a question

Asking a question gets your prospect involved with your ad. And if you word it right, it will confirm that you have what they're looking for.

362. Target by geographical area

If your clients are located in a specific area, mention the name of the area in your ad.

363. Boost your credibility

If you have room, include something that boosts your credibility (such as a five-star rating or membership of a recognised industry body).

364. Avoid superlatives

Words are limited in PPC ads so don't waste space with vague, meaningless, and overused words like 'amazing', 'fantastic' or 'unbelievable'.

365. Use power words that will trigger an emotional response

Examples: latest, ultimate, master, scientific, private, discount, cheap, wholesale, special, massive, leading, outstanding, rebate, coupon, guaranteed, free, powerful, easy, shocking, hidden, proven, revolutionary, inside, hot, new, improved, breakthrough, limited, secrets.

366. Back up your claims on your landing page

For example, if your PPC ad states that your product is considered the best in the market, prove it on your landing page.

To apply for a free implementation session **worth £495** where we show you how everything in this book can be done for you, go to **completedigitalmarketingsystem.com/121**

125

367. Add a call to action to your link

Get a little creative with your calls to action (but not so much that visitors are confused).

Try any of these:

- Buy today
- Call today
- Get a free quote
- Reserve your spot now
- Read reviews
- Request information

368. Mention any free stuff included in your offer

Free is still a big incentive online so make sure you mention whatever you're giving away in your PPC ad. For example, "Free shipping", "Free 30-day trial", "Free report", "Buy one get one free."

369. Give your reader a reason to buy ASAP

If your sale ends soon, mention it. If availability is limited, let your reader know. Try to create a sense of urgency.

370. Avoid making general claims

Instead of saying "great tasting peaches", say "7-time winner of the Tasty Peach award".

371. Use the brand name

If the brand you're promoting is well-known and has a great reputation, use the name in your ad.

372. Keep your URL short

As a rule of thumb, the shorter the URL the better. If possible, test several different ones. If your URL contains at least one of your keywords, it will give you an edge in getting your ad clicked. (As an added bonus, the keyword part of your URL will be bolded in the ad.)

373. The ad must be ultra-relevant

This might seem obvious, but if your PPC ad says "shoes" don't send prospects to a landing page that sells socks. You'll not only be blowing potential sales, you'll lose money every time someone interested in shoes clicks on the ad.

374. Make sure your ad lives up to your prospect's expectations

It has to be *immediately* apparent to your prospect that, having clicked on your ad, they've landed in the right place. Your landing page must relate to your ad and the keyphrase the prospect used to find it.

375. Update your negative keyword list

Using negative keywords is one of the main ways to improve your campaign. Before you start any campaign, look at all potential negative keywords and decide which will work best for you. Constantly review your negative keyword list to save money on useless clicks and to increase your campaign's conversion rate.

376. Look at the combination of keywords

When you review your keywords, you'll get an idea of how many broad or phrase match terms are being used. If most of them are broad match, one way to get control of your cost and revenue is to add phrase match and exact match terms.

Be sure to monitor what you are showing up for in order to optimise your account accordingly. Click on keywords and then details, to retrieve the search query report that shows exactly what keywords are working so you can exclude or include them.

377. Group ad groups by topics

The more specific you group your campaigns and ad groups, the greater their relevancy and the better the quality score. This will positively affect your performance. Eliminate ad groups that include keywords covering too many topics and organise them into segmented groups. Also, make sure to create tailored landing pages per ad group.

378. Consistently test landing pages and advertisements

To continuously improve ad performance, test what works best on a regular basis. For example, if your landing page has a low conversion rate, e.g. 1%, create a copy of that page and make small changes. The trick is to make small changes one at a time so you are able to pinpoint what changes work.

You can also pause all ads but the top three performing ads (per ad group that is) and then write new ad copies to test against your top three for two weeks.

Experts are divided when it comes to ad optimisation because some think the top performing ad is the one with the highest CTR and the conversion rate is just determined by the landing page, whilst others think it's a combination of ad text and landing page.

Optimise the ads based on conversion rate and run small landing page tests.

379. Be aware of the importance of landing pages

Landing pages can significantly boost your quality score, reduce your cost per click, and improve the customers' experience. Simultaneously, good landing pages have a lower bounce rate. All of these factors come together to create a higher return on investment.

380. Find out where things are going wrong

Discover where you are losing the majority of your impressions. Review the impression share statistics to see how much market share – meaning the percentage of all possible impressions for the keywords you are advertising with – you currently have.

On the campaigns tab, click the customise columns button above the graph in your AdWords account and add "Impression Share (lost due to budget)" and "Impression Share (lost due to rank)" under the "Competitive Metrics" category.

- If your impressions are lost due to budget, you are hitting your daily spending 'cap'. Once this cap is reached, your ads won't be shown, and your competitors are free to take over. If this is happening, it's worth increasing your daily budget if possible.

- If your impressions are lost due to rank, your budget is fine but the ad position is too low to get the maximum impressions that are available in the market place. In this case, try new ad copies and split test landing pages to increase the quality score. You can also increase keywords bids.

381. Optimise your performance with display network placements

Like a keyword report, a placement report helps you with identifying the placements or sites where your ads were displayed. Of course not all these placements would be relevant to the product you sell or the service you offer. Eliminate sites that produce low or no profit. By pausing less profitable placements, you will have more budget available for the most profitable placements.

382. Evaluate performance by device and optimise bid based on margins

Make sure that you regularly run your "segmentation by device report" and look at every ad group. By performing this analysis periodically, you can keep your campaigns running more efficiently across all devices.

Don't forget to integrate Google Analytics. It's a great way to compare mobile and desktop users and it provides you with enough data to tailor your communication strategy.

383. Adjust bids per geographic location and based on actual results

There are two ways of adjusting your bid per geographic location. One is to simply create one campaign per country. This will also enable you to analyse conversions by the hour of the day because you have fewer time zones to deal with.

The second way to do it is to target multiple locations in one campaign, and to adjust the bid in the campaign settings. Click on "locations" and set up your bid variation percentages for each location you are targeting.

You can also exclude locations that you don't service or are not interested in getting inquiries from. If radius-targeting is being used, make sure it targets an accurate range surrounding your location.

384. Analyse conversion rate by day and hour

Are there profitable or unprofitable hours of the day? Maybe you are not converting at all at 10am but get half of your daily conversions at 3pm. You can use the Ads and Keywords segmented reports by pulling a report for your indicated time period, then clicking on the report button and adding a segment for Day. You can even go as far as segmenting for Time. Export this data into Excel or Numbers and determine what days receive the most traffic and clicks, and what days receive the least. Adjust bid scheduling accordingly, or determine if there are days that can be taken out of the schedule.

385. Use ad extensions

Make certain your campaigns have ad extensions such as 'services offered' or the traditional 'about us' and 'contact' tabs. Why? It's a free tool to increase your CTR. If you are unsure what extensions to use, start with site links. Also consider location extension and call extension.

386. Not tracking ads and keywords is a costly mistake

If keywords and ads aren't performing, you're wasting money. You can use the free Google Analytics tool to help you track activity. Keywords should also be tested and tracked with misspellings, plurals and stemming options.

387. Apply the "conversion code"

Be sure to apply the "conversion code," which is a simple JavaScript set that goes into your landing page or thank you page. This information will show up in a column on your AdWords dashboard when you log in, and is a quick way to check for lead counts and important for tracking return on spend.

388. Do turn off the 'content network'

When first setting up a campaign, turn off the 'content network'. This is a default option and a form of contextual advertising. You typically will see high impressions in your system, but often low CTR (click-through-rates), as determined by impressions to clicks – and low-quality clicks. These aren't serious buyers; they're wasting your money and time.

389. Don't use too many keywords

When creating new campaigns and ad groups, many people begin by entering every keyword under the sun. Don't. Targeting is key; think about your niche and the categories within it. You can use free suggestion tools to determine which keywords to begin with.

390. Don't ignore quality score and its impact on costs

Quality score is a scale of 1-10 of how relevant your site, ads and keywords are to a searcher. The more aligned those three elements are, the higher the quality score.

Campaigns with high quality scores pay less per click and get placed higher in the ad placements.

Look for keywords in your campaign that rank a 4 or lower. Consider updating your ad for that keyword and the page on your website that ad is pointing to.

All three elements should be representing the same idea.

391. Do use Google Analytics

AdWords gets visitors to your website. Google Analytics tells you what they did once they got there.

Google Analytics is a free product so there's no excuse not to do this.

By connecting the two services (which is easy to do if you're an administrator of both services) you'll get to see more detailed data about each of your campaigns.

- Are visitors via AdWords bouncing off your page as soon as they get there?

- Are visitors via AdWords engaging with your content?

By seeing some of these data points you can make more informed decisions about campaigns.

392. Clicks do not equal customers

If you're getting lots of clicks but no leads or sales, you're losing money hand over fist. The only one profiting from that situation is Google.

Instead of aiming for clicks, your goal should be to attract new paying customers or clients, and to earn a healthy return on investment from your advertising.

393. Track your results – even if you think you're doing well

If you're not tracking, you're flying blind. You have no idea whether your ads are profitable or unprofitable… and most likely, you're losing money every month. You should always track your advertising. Even if your ads are generating an ROI, you should be tracking so you can improve your ROI.

394. Put your top benefit in the first line of your ad and top feature in the second

Place the biggest benefit of your product or service in the first line of your ad. Put the most important feature of your product or service in the second line.

395. Make the offer in your ad irresistible

Create an irresistible offer. Your offer should differentiate you from your competition and give you a huge advantage. Most importantly, if truly irresistible, it should help your ad to generate more responses.

You need people to respond immediately rather than later – because later often means never. Anything you can do to give them an extra reason to take action now will make your advertising more effective and profitable.

An irresistible offer consists of the following core components:

- Defined value: your product or service must be more valuable than the price, and the value has to be clear to your potential customers. That doesn't mean your offer has to be cheap, however.

- Reason for offer: a reason for your offer eliminates scepticism and suspicion, which is always present when you make an offer that appears to be too good to be true.

- Call to action: ask for the sale. The best way to generate response is with a deadline. Deadlines can either be time-based (offer expires on a specified date) or quantity-based (limited supply).

396. Great ads will save you money as well as boost responses

Google's AdWords auction-based bidding system rewards you for writing great ads that get clicked more than your competition. With the right ads, you can save a lot of money.

397. Focus your ad on one idea

You may have several selling points you'd like to cram into your ad, but resist the temptation to squeeze them all in. Instead, focus your ad around one big idea. That may be the big benefit your product or service provides, or it may be the big thing that differentiates you from your competitors.

To apply for a free implementation session **worth £495** where we show you how everything
in this book can be done for you, go to **completedigitalmarketingsystem.com/121**

133

398. Create your landing page with the end in mind

You need to send people from your ad to a special landing page (not your homepage). To create a compelling landing page, start with the end in mind. That is, know exactly what action you want prospects to take on that page.

Even if there are several things you want people to do, pick the most important one, and make that the focus of your landing page.

399. Make the call to action on your landing page completely obvious

When you're designing the layout of your landing page, make sure you allocate proportionate space and attention to the action you want people to take. Don't leave any doubt in your website visitors' minds. If possible, put your call to action at the top of the page, so people can see it without scrolling down.

Try this test: Stand 5-10 feet away from your computer monitor and see if you can still understand what you're supposed to do on your landing page.

400. Conversion is more important than traffic

If you can double your conversion rate, you'll double your sales without increasing your traffic and without increasing your ad spend.

Chapter 5

Use Education Marketing for Lead Generation

In a Nutshell

Ninety-eight percent of the people who visit your website will leave without taking any action. Most who come aren't actually looking to buy anything yet. They're simply looking for information. Unfortunately, once they leave, they're unlikely to ever return.

But what if there was a method of capturing the interest of those 'just browsing' visitors –so much so that they gave you their names and contact details?

Education marketing is that method. It is a way of delivering the information your prospective customers are looking for.

Why would you bother? After all, you're in it to make money, aren't you?

Yes, and this will bring in money, but not immediately. When you give your website visitors information, you start to create a relationship with them. They start to perceive you as someone who knows what they're talking about. You become known as an expert in your area.

If they really like your information, they'll return to your website. They may even share your information with other people, just like them. Which means, they are expanding your marketing reach for you. For free.

There's another strong reason to 'educate' your prospective customers: educated consumers make the best customers. Research[2] shows that customers who engage with a company's educational marketing offerings are 29 times more likely to purchase a company's product than those who are informed through media ads alone, and five times more likely to make a purchase than those reached by direct marketing. They are also 94% more satisfied with their purchase and 93% more likely to tell friends about their experience.

Done well, your education marketing offerings – things such as information guides, books, special reports, white papers, case studies, articles – should not appear to be pushing your products or services. Instead, prospects should feel as if your sole purpose is to help them achieve success with their objectives and pursuits.

This will help to build trust, loyalty and credibility with customers, which directly translates to increased customer retention and higher revenues. Use the following tips to position yourself as a "trusted advisor".

401. Focus on delivering high quality content to your prospects

That will demonstrate that you are a source of useful information and also keep them coming back for more.

402. Your content is your salesperson

Your content does all the work of a salesperson on behalf of you and your company. And it costs you nothing.

403. Know who your customers are and what they want

Before you start creating any educational marketing material, get to know your target market. You need to find out:

- What your prospective customers want

- How they make buying decisions

---

[2] Harvey, Bill, 'Consumer Education Produced High ROI', Next Century Media, 2006.

- What information and learning opportunities are they seeking that you can provide?

404. Understand your competitive market space

What are your competitors up to? How are they positioning and branding themselves? Are they employing an educational marketing strategy? If so, is their strategy effective? How can you differentiate from your competitors in a way that reinforces your brand message?

405. Write a book or information guide

Writing a book or information guide is the best way to establish your credibility in your field of expertise. Using authorship as a marketing strategy brings you an ongoing flow of clients who are deliberately and purposefully seeking you.

406. You don't have to be a great writer to produce a great business book

Your book doesn't have to be a masterpiece to get across what you want to say. It just needs to give your prospective customers or clients information they want to solve a problem. That's it.

407. Writing a book doesn't have to take years

The book you need to write to attract customers is something that you should be able to write (or have someone else write for you) in a matter of weeks rather than months or years.

408. You don't need to find a publisher or an agent to create a book

You can publish your own book very easily and quickly these days without needing an agent or publisher. You can publish an informative, authoritative book in a very short amount of time for a nominal cost.

409. Use your first book solely as a marketing tool

You need to think of your book as a marketing tool to build your reputation as the obvious expert. Your goal is to get something in print and use the right distribution channels to get it to your target audience.

410. You don't have to know everything in the world about your subject matter

You just have to know more than your readers know about your subject.

411. Don't worry about revealing too much information

Some people worry that if they write an informative book that clients will no longer need them. Most people will be too lazy or busy to actually use the information in your book. That's fine. They'll come to you to do it all for them.

412. The more you give away, the more you'll get back

The more information you reveal in your book or information guide, the more respect, trust, and loyalty you will earn from your readers. If they love your material, they will be more likely to rave about it to their friends and contacts. Remember, the best advertisement for your business is a happy customer. The worst advertisement for your business is an unhappy customer.

413. Narrow your subject matter

Pick one piece of one subject that you think you know more about than most people know. "How to" topics especially lend themselves to this type of writing.

414. Test your idea in the real world

Your employees may tell you the topic you've chosen to write about is a sure winner. Your mum may tell you it's going to be a "runaway success". But the only way you can be sure you've chosen a topic prospects will be interested in is to ask them. Survey them. If the topic you've chosen is a stinker, it's better to find out before you've committed any time or energy to it.

415. Don't wait for 'creativity' to hit

Once you've found the right topic and know what you want to say, just start writing. Sit down at the computer, write longhand on a piece of paper, or speak into a digital recorder. It doesn't have to be perfect or organised.

416. You can always hire someone to write for you

You can pay a ghost-writer to create your book. They will turn your knowledge and thoughts into a cohesive format ready to publish. When published, the book will bear your name as the author. If you need this kind of support, you might be surprised at how easily this alternative can be put into action.

417. Give your book away for free

One of the easiest ways to use a book to become the expert in your field is to give the book away. As a consultant or coach for example, you can send your book – along with a cover letter – to the top 500 CEOs of companies who are perfect prospects for buying your consulting or professional services.

418. Research will help boost your expertise

When you write a book on any subject, you're forced to do additional research – and this will help you to increase your knowledge in your chosen niche.

419. If you're not yet an expert, interview people who are experts

If you're fairly new in your niche and don't have a ton of experience, interview the people who are. The association with those experts will give you credibility.

Once you've decided on your book's angle, create a 'wish list' of 'thought leaders' in your area, market or industry that you'd like to interview for your book. Make contact with them and ask them if they will agree to be interviewed for your book. Some will refuse. It doesn't matter. Go with the ones who agree. Have your questions prepared. Record the interview. Get it transcribed. Make sure you include the names of the experts in your book blurb and in all your promotional material.

420. Save yourself tons of time: don't write what you think your market wants to read about

You probably have the perfect idea for your first book, information guide, white paper or special report. Write the title down. Maybe go as far as creating a cover with that title and your name underneath. Save that file. Close it. Now go and find out what your prospective customers or clients are *actually* interested in. Only ever write stuff that your readers care about and you'll save yourself a ton of time and effort.

421. Organising your book will help you in other areas of your business

When you write a book, you're also forced to organise your material into a logical sequence. Doing this will help you to clarify how to present your material in other settings – for example, in your consulting sessions, workshops, seminars and speeches.

422. You can recycle the information in your book

Your book can be the basis for a seminar or workshop. Your chapters can become modules in the seminar or workshop. You can use parts of chapters as articles or blog posts. You can package up a chapter into a special report.

423. Your book will help you attract more clients and sell more products

Potential clients reading your book will call you to inquire about the services you offer and will be predisposed to hire you.

424. As an author, you're more likely to get invitations to speak

Associations will ask you to speak at their conferences for generous fees if you are the author of a book that interests their members.

425. Being an author boosts your status

Listing yourself as the author of a book is an impressive credential on your website, brochure and other marketing materials. It increases your status.

- You can give copies of your book to potential clients to familiarise them with your methodology and convince them that you are an expert in your field.

- Editors will ask you to contribute articles to their publications.

- The media will want to interview you as an expert in your field. This can lead to guest appearances on radio and TV shows.

426. Your clients can help you to write your book

Ask your prospective readers the biggest questions/challenges/ issues they have about your subject. You'll need between 100 and 150 questions. Once you've gathered those questions, sort through them, and find the 12 most critical questions/challenges/issues.

These 12 questions will become a chapter in your book. Break each chapter into four subchapters. You'll end up with 48 different sections: 12 main chapters with four subsections each.

Then simply answer your prospective readers' questions.

427. Create an outline before you start writing

Many people begin writing by creating an outline. This is a great way to lay out the points you want to make. Work on one section at a time.

428. Write how you talk

Just imagine you're sitting in front of someone and want to teach or explain something important to them. You can go back later to reorganise it and tidy it up.

429. Chunk it down

It's easy to get overwhelmed if you keep thinking of how many thousands of words you need to write. Get over this hurdle by breaking the task down into do-able chunks. For example, if you have to write 900 words on a point in your book, think how you can break that point down into three smaller sub-points of say, 300 words each.

430. Keep your writing reader-oriented

It's easy to get sidetracked but your book should be focused completely on your reader. Keep every sentence reader-focused. Think, "Will the reader really care about this? Why? Why not?"

431. Write in the active rather than the passive voice

The active voice makes for stronger and more effective statements. It's also more engaging and interesting to read.

432. Be ruthless when it comes to editing your work

When it comes to editing your work, you have to put aside the fact you sweated blood to reach your word count. You have to be ruthless. Does it make sense? Is there a paragraph or a chapter that doesn't quite work? If there is, rewrite it. Have you got your point across? Is there are a better way of saying something?

433. Write to one person rather than many

Write as if you're talking to one person rather than a group. Make it personal. Use the word 'you' so your readers really feel as if your book is addressing them directly.

434. Write the introduction to your book or information guide last

After you've written the main part of your book, go back to write your introduction. The introduction should simply tell your reader what he or she will discover inside the book. What it will do for them. What they will be able to do once they've read it. Use your introduction to whet the appetite of your reader.

435. Write the conclusion after you've written your introduction

The conclusion should be a short and punchy summary of what you've said in the book. It should make your reader feel good after reading your book, and filled with hope and optimism that they can do what you just showed them.

436. Your information guide will help you sell more

The information guide you write contributes to the selling process in two ways: first, by predisposing readers to accept your methods as standard and desirable; second, by positioning you and your firm as experts in the topic.

437. The success of your information guide or book depends on your title

The title of your book or information guide is crucial because it determines, in large part, whether you can get prospects interested enough to send for it. So choose the title with care.

438. Choose a targeted topic and title

When choosing a topic and title, it's better to make it narrow and more targeted than broad and general. By narrowing the focus, you can cover one specific topic of great interest to your prospects with sufficient detail to gain their attention and whet their appetite for further contact with you.

439. Give your book or guide an intriguing title

Title your book or information guide with something that piques readers' curiosity, and entices them to read more.

440. Use a descriptive subtitle

If you worry that a title based more on intrigue won't give enough context to attract a would-be reader, use a descriptive subtitle to spell out what the book or information guides delivers.

441. Use keywords in your subtitle

A descriptive subtitle is a good place to affix search terms or keywords that your would-be readers are monitoring and searching for.

442. Put a price on the front or back cover of your information guide or book

This serves a couple of functions:

- It adds to the perceived value of the booklet or report; people are more interested in getting a £12.97 item for free than they are in getting a free item for free.

- It allows you to request payment gracefully from the occasional person who calls you up and wants multiple copies for a seminar, presentation, class, or to distribute in some other fashion. This does happen every once in a while, and it can be costly.

443. For initial interactions, a top tips report is better than a book

When you're at the first stages of turning a prospect into a customer, you want to present information that is easily digestible. A top tips report is perfect for this.

444. The contents do not have to be revolutionary or give the reader all new information

Many people read to affirm current beliefs or reinforce existing knowledge. So even if your book or guide mostly repeats what they already know, they'll be happy with it, and, more importantly, they'll think you're a wise, knowledgeable expert on the topic.

However, if you can give readers one or two genuinely new ideas or things they may not have thought of before, so much the better. It will make your book or guide even more valuable to them.

445. Don't put any selling or advertising message into the body of the book

The contents should be pure information. You have promised readers knowledge; you impress them by conveying that knowledge. If you turn the book into a sales pitch, the people who sent for it expecting helpful advice will be angry, disappointed, turned off and not inclined to do business with you.

446. How much information you include will depend on your topic

How much should you write? Just enough to cover the topic and deliver on the promise you made.

447. Make your information guide or report helpful and fascinating, but don't overdo the detail

Tell prospects enough to get them interested in hiring you or buying your product to solve their problem. You don't need to give away every secret you've ever discovered in your working life.

448. Get a client to read your book or information guide before you publish

When you finish your information guide or book, ask a client to read it for you. Tell them you'd appreciate their honest feedback. Say you want to know that it makes sense. Does it address a need that people like them have? Are there are parts that jar or don't work well?

Don't get discouraged if the feedback is not as positive as you'd hoped. Just use it to improve your writing.

449. Set aside time every day to write

Be disciplined about writing your book or information guide by setting aside time every day to work on it. Treat it the same way you would any important business task. After all, once completed, it will help you to build your business.

450. Don't edit as you write

Look at a point you want to write about. Set your timer for three minutes. Just write about that one point for three minutes. Don't worry about style, spelling, or grammar – just get the words on the page. You can always go back and edit your work later.

451. Know when to stop writing and publish

While making your book or information guide something you can be proud of is important, there's a point where you have to let it go. Don't keep tweaking it. Publish it. You can always start working on the next one.

452. Offer your readers something enticing at the end of the book

At the back of your book, offer your readers something they'll find irresistible: a discount on their next purchase or a free telephone consultation, for example. Make it clear that it's a reader's only offer. Put a deadline on the offer to encourage them to take immediate action. Or say that it's only available for the first 20 people to respond. Give booking or discount codes to add credibility to your offer.

453. Tell readers how to take action on your offer

If you offer readers something at the end of the book (and you should), tell them exactly what they need to do to get it. So, if you want them to call, provide the telephone number. Tell them to call it. If you want them to go to a landing page, give them the URL address and tell them to put the address into their web browser. It's better in this situation to provide too much rather than not enough information. What you don't want to happen is for your reader to get confused and not take the desired action.

454. Make sure you have the resources in place to cope when people accept the offer

If you offer readers a free telephone consultation, make sure that you have space in your diary to accommodate them. If you offer them a discount on their next purchase or booking, make sure procedures are in place to accept their booking or discount codes.

455. Have a professional take care of your book's layout rather than doing it yourself

Unless you're a trained graphic designer or typesetter, hire a professional to take care of your book's layout. The book will look a gazillion times better for it.

456. Use plenty of white space to give your content breathing room

Your content will appear more visually pleasing when it's surrounded by plenty of white space. Squashed type looks ugly and makes it hard to see key points. (Or even care what they are!)

457. Create a hyperlinked table of contents

If you're offering PDFs of any of your content, make sure the table of contents is live – that is, each chapter heading or section is hotlinked to the corresponding text. When referencing something else online, be sure to hyperlink to it so that your readers can find out more.

458. Encourage sharing with social media

Encourage readers to share your content with their social media network.

Make it easy for them to share your white papers, information guides, special reports, case studies, best practice guides–after all, when done right, these can be powerful lead generation and lead nurturing tools.

The mere presence of email and social media sharing buttons in PDFs may prompt readers to share the PDF with others when they otherwise wouldn't have even thought about doing so, says Galen De Young, a content marketing specialist[3].

---

[3] De Young, Galen, 'Do Your PDFs Have Embedded Sharing Options?', MarketingProfs.com, September 15, 2009.

To apply for a free implementation session **worth £495** where we show you how everything in this book can be done for you, go to **completedigitalmarketingsystem.com/121**

147

459. The easier you make it for people to share your content, the more likely they are to do it

Make sure the email and social media sharing options you embed in PDFs populate information in the target social media. Do the same for email sharing options. For instance, if you want people to tweet about your PDF, don't just have the sharing button in your PDF launch Twitter for them. Have it launch Twitter and populate the tweet for them.

They can change the tweet if they want, but at least they'll have a starting point from which to make edits. If the person is fine with the pre-populated tweet, the entire social media sharing process could take them as little as five seconds.

If you pre-populate the tweet for people, include your shortened URL, you'll be able to better track results through bit.ly, HootSuite, or whatever you use.

Pre-populating information in the target social media can result in better click-through.

460. Track the results of your content being shared on social media

Quantifying traffic from social media referral sources like LinkedIn and Facebook is fairly simple. Using your web analytics, you can look at the referral sources for the landing page on which your PDF is hosted.

Tracking results from Twitter is a bit more difficult. If you pre-populate the reader's tweet for them, you can specify the shortened URL to be used in the tweet. Most URL shortening services have tracking data available. Just make sure you're logged into your URL shortening service account when you shorten the URL so you'll have access to the tracking for that shortened URL.

The tracking data available from your URL shortening service will tell you how many people clicked on the shortened URL, but it won't tell you what those people did once they got to your site.

461. It makes sense to embed sharing options in your online content

Without sharing options, you have to rely more heavily on sales staff, public relations, paid search, and SEO to drive awareness and use. Further, embedding sharing options not only helps with the launch of new content marketing assets, but it also helps perpetuate their visibility as new people find and share them long after they've been released. Finally, social media sharing options in PDFs help encourage and make it easy for B2B buyers in particular to share your information with others involved in a particular purchase decision.

462. Keep the end in mind when creating any educational material

Remember, the ultimate aim of educational marketing is to get more customers. Keep that in mind and use it as an incentive to carry on writing when things get hard.

463. Use article marketing:

Article marketing is one of the most effective promotional methods to publicise your website and to increase the number of back links (incoming links) to your website content. To ensure ongoing awareness, articles should be submitted to suitable article directories, and content publishers.

464. Write relevant online articles

Writing articles and getting them published in online article directories or on other people's websites or blogs is a great way to encourage prospective clients to visit your website, while at the same time demonstrating your expertise in your niche market.

For that to happen your articles must address some of the challenges that your prospective clients face and provide information they want.

465. Expand your reach with articles

Place your articles in print media and on the web. This can be on your own website as well as anywhere else in need of quality content.

466. Consider the editor's point of view

If you want to get your article published in a print magazine or in a digital magazine, make sure it conforms to the publication's requirements (length, tone, style, etc.) and is of immediate interest to its readers.

467. Make sure every article you write contains three essential elements

The following are the essential elements of any article:

- The headline: use a headline that grabs your prospects' attention.

- Valuable content: create useful, valuable, and relevant information that helps readers.

- A resource box: this should include a call to action. You need to give readers a compelling reason to click the link at the end of the article.

468. Write problem/solution articles

People online are mainly searching for solutions to their problems. So, if you do effective keyword research and write problem/solution articles, your articles will be found on the search engines when prospects type in their problems that need fixing.

The trick is to only give a little bit of the how so they'll want to go back to your website to discover the whole solution.

469. Write right and wrong articles

If you were engaging in an activity and someone told you that there's a right way and a wrong way, wouldn't you want to know if you were in the right or in the wrong? Well, so do your prospects. This is the best way to let them know in a nice way that they're wrong AND that you're the person best placed to help them.

470. Write articles with a negative slant

Articles with a negative slant are more likely to grab people's attention than those with a positive slant. They're also more likely to be shared. Just because they have a negative slant doesn't mean you can't include a positive message. You can.

471. Write 'how to' articles

'How to' articles are the most popular kind of articles online. People love them. Break a process down into easy steps and turn that into an article ("Two easy steps to write a 'how to' article", for example).

472. Use keywords in your article headings

To ensure your article gets indexed by the search engines and seen by your prospects, you must use the keywords that your prospects use to find a service like yours. However, you need to maintain a balance between keyword density (the number of times a keyword is used within an article to get a high ranking on search engines) and readability. If hyperlinks are allowed, include them in and around keyphrases throughout your article.

473. Write special reports

Once you know the questions your clients ask, develop some special reports that address those questions. A special report is a great way to deliver educational material. It is inexpensive to create and distribute, and brands you as an expert information resource as well as someone who has shared a valuable free gift.

474. Keep the special report short

You need to keep in mind that the information you present to prospects should be easily digestible. You want to keep it short, but you also want to take care that you include solid, useful information that your client will find helpful.

475. Write your special report like a journalist not a fiction writer

Special reports are written in journalistic style-much the same way a feature article would be written for a major news magazine. They generally focus on just one topic. The purpose of your report is to provide valuable information that your client couldn't get anywhere else. This will reinforce your value and integrity in the mind of your client.

476. Use examples in your special report to bring it alive

Be sure to include real life stories that drive home important points. This will create interest and keep your client reading.

477. Include all your contact information in your special report

Make it easy for people to make contact with you by including all your contact information like your full name, business address, phone numbers and website address.

478. Always put a price on the cover of your free reports

Even though you give them away for free, people will value them more and be more apt to hold on to those items.

479. Get a strategic or joint venture partner to promote your special report

Boost interest in your special report by sending it with a cover letter signed by your strategic or joint venture partner urging the client to read it.

Your joint-venture partner can also distribute the special report in their shop, office or send it via a PDF file and distribute it over the internet.

Have your joint venture partner send an email announcing the free special report you've developed for his clients then point readers to a web page to view and download it.

480. Focus your special report on a very specific problem your readers want to solve

Make your topic as narrow as possible. Your special report should provide specific step-by-step directions on how to meet those objectives.

Possible subject matter for special reports includes:

- New procedures that you have created and which have worked well for your clients

- Statistical up-to-the-minute data, which your readership would normally not have access to

- Trends and forecasts

- Case studies and success stories

- Resources you are aware of that would be helpful to your clients.

481. Understand the benefits of special reports

Special reports position you as an expert in your area. They also provide you with an opportunity to up-sell your products or services.

482. You don't need to write your special report

It doesn't matter if you don't consider yourself a 'writer' or simply don't have the time to do it – you can outsource the research and the writing quite easily. What's more, you can put your name on the cover once it's complete.

483. You can also repurpose your special report

Edit it down into a number of short articles and publish them online. Or use them as blog posts on your website.

484. Encourage feedback in your special report

Invite readers to get in contact with you if they have questions and to keep you updated on their progress.

485. Use your blog posts as chapters in your book or sections in your special report

If you create regular blog posts, you may have enough content for a book or special report. Look at what you've written. See if you can develop any of your blog posts into slightly longer pieces, long enough to be chapters.

486. Create communities

Develop a microsite or Facebook fan page to create communities around your book.

487. Conduct an audit of your existing content

You may have already created enough content for a book. At the very least, you may have the foundations for all your chapters. Go through everything you've written to see what you can repurpose.

488. Consider co-authoring a book

Are there business owners who target the same prospects and customers you do but who you don't consider direct competition? Consider approaching them to co-author a book with you. That will halve your workload but double your potential network.

489. Clarify what you want readers to get from your book

Keep the purpose of your book in mind throughout the creation process. As you write, keep asking yourself, "Will this help serve my book's purpose? Will it help my reader?"

490. Consider creating an audiobook

Audiobooks are very popular and present an ideal way for you to reach your audience. Use the content from your book and offer it in mp3 format or on a CD. Unless you have a fantastic voice, consider hiring a professional to narrate your book – it will make it a more pleasurable listening experience.

491. Develop your strategy for distribution

How will you get your information guide, special report, white paper or article to your prospects? Plan how you'll do this before you create your marketing piece.

492. Make liberal use of visual elements

Solid blocks of text can be off-putting even to the most committed reader. Provide bullet points, callouts, sidebars, graphs, etc. in all your content.

493. You can use video to transmit educational content

Create videos that convey information your prospects will find useful, interesting, and entertaining. Place them on your website and on your YouTube channel. Share them on other sites like Vimeo too. All the video sites provide social media options to allow commenting and sharing which will help with the distribution of your video.

494. Use a professional presenter for your video

Performing well in front of a camera is difficult for most people and it takes time to build the confidence you need. The last thing you want is to appear nervous. Avoid this by getting a professional presenter to do your video for you.

495. Aim for a video series rather than a one-off

Don't stop at one video. Create a series of videos that build interest and an audience over time.

496. Make sure the audio on your video is top-notch

The most important part of a video is the audio quality. A bad audio track can make even an Oscar-worthy film excruciating to watch. Again, get professionals to help you create a high quality audio track.

497. If you're a B2B business, create white papers

White papers are topical reports, usually about eight to 12 pages long. They're also known as conference papers, research reports, or technical briefs. They're a great way to demonstrate your expertise on issues that matter to your prospective clients. White papers provide a high return on engagement for almost any B2B company.

Prospects who are in the early stages of the sales cycle are the ones who frequently register in order to download white papers. In fact, it's been shown that white papers can offer higher interest and better conversion than free trials, analyst reports, and even webinars.

498. White papers will help grow your business

Once created, white papers can really help to grow your business. That's because white papers can generate leads, position the company as a thought leader and can be created in print, PDF or digital magazine format (which gives them a wide reach).

499. White papers have wings

White papers are frequently passed around to many people in an organisation, which is particularly useful when your business relies on more than one person to make buying decisions. Your white paper can be a way of reaching a key decision maker who would be otherwise hard to make contact with.

500. Don't sell in your white paper

Your white paper should feature well-researched, substantive content that steers clear of selling. Begin with a discussion on the major issues or problems, and line them up with a need faced by the reader.

Provide some solid learning; try to teach prospects something they may not have known and show benefits that they may not have been aware of.

501. Promote your white paper everywhere

Place the white paper on your website in exchange for prospect contact information. Promote it via syndication networks, which will distribute it through a network of specialty, vertically oriented websites that are targeted based on your ideal lead.

To apply for a free implementation session **worth £495** where we show you how everything in this book can be done for you, go to **completedigitalmarketingsystem.com/121**

Chapter 6

Social Media – Facebook Marketing

In a Nutshell

You need to be where your target audience is and internet users spend a huge amount of time on social media sites, particularly Facebook, Twitter, and LinkedIn.

With over one billion members (and about 750,000,000 unique monthly visitors), Facebook is still the most popular social network and can be used by marketers to reach consumers in nearly any industry.

Facebook captures 10% of all internet visits, with visitors spending an average of 28 minutes on the site. Even more revealing, 50% of Facebook fans prefer brand pages to company websites.

Naturally enough, where customers go, businesses follow. Research reveals that 41% of B2B companies and 62% of B2C companies have acquired a customer from Facebook. By being present on this site, you are taking back some of the control in your marketing by giving your potential future customers a new channel to discover you on.

The 2013 Social Media Marketing Industry Report said the top two benefits of social media marketing are increasing exposure and increasing traffic. A significant 89% of all marketers indicated that their social media efforts have generated more exposure for their businesses. Increasing traffic was the second major benefit, with 75% reporting positive results.

In the UK, 72.7% of Facebook's 33 million UK monthly users come back every day.

At least 25 million small businesses have active company pages. One million companies advertise on Facebook, which means that only 4% of companies that use Facebook to connect with customers are also using the site to advertise.

The following tips will help you to get the best possible use out of Facebook.

502. Have a plan

Find out where your customers and prospects are having conversations and where your business can add value. Google alerts can be used effectively for this purpose.

503. Don't worry about being perfect

Start by listening and learning from others. It's perfectly acceptable to be a 'newbie' – and people are usually happy to help you.

504. Focus on one social media channel at a time

It is much better to be effective using one social media tool than to use five of them poorly. Choose the tool based on where most of your customers and prospects are.

505. Keep a look out for emerging platforms

It's beneficial to keep an eye out for emerging platforms, but make sure that you don't do this at the expense of Facebook, which is typically the most effective.

506. Be consistent

If you can only spend one hour a week, be there consistently for that period of time. This is a much better strategy than spending three hours one day and then 15 minutes the next week.

507. Don't spend too long on Facebook

Social media can gobble up your time so allot a fixed amount of time each day to Facebook posts and responses and stick to it. It is easy to get distracted, especially with social media, and begin to drift. Get on and get off the social media tool according to your plan.

508. Use your own voice online

This should reflect you and your company brand. All consumers now value the human voice.

509. Turn off notifications

These are time interrupters and will decrease your overall productivity when you are not working on social media.

510. Schedule new content posts

Optimally, this would be on a weekly basis to start.

511. Review analytics

Every marketing activity needs to have a result. This is no different.

512. Set an expected return on your investment

What does your business hope to gain from social media over what period of time?

513. Watch and learn before you take part

Before you leap in with comments, posts, contributions, check out how things work. Spend a few hours or more reading, watching and listening to learn how things work. Monitor social media conversations that are happening around you, what others in your industry or competitors are doing, and what your customers are saying.

514. Engage users by posting content that your audience will want to read and care about

When you post content, be sure to include a link, photo, video or even ask a question – something to give your audience a reason to act and respond. Retweet, repost or engage with others. You can't expect someone to engage with you and your business if you're not willing to do the same thing.

515. Ask questions

If you want to encourage discussion, ask a question. There are lott of different types of questions you can ask. To ask a question or poll on Facebook, use the 'Question' link under your Page's 'Share' options. If you like, you can convert your question into a poll by selecting 'Add poll options'.

516. Questions give you insights about your audience

Questions about your brand, product, or service stimulate discussion, but they're also useful for the insights they can give you about your audience. Asking questions on Facebook, according to research from Social Media Scientist Dan Zarrella, is an excellent way to generate more comments. Just keep in mind that while questions do encourage comments, they tend to garner fewer 'likes' and 'shares'.

517. Ask open-ended questions

Ask questions that require more than a "yes" or "no" response.

518. Engage customers by holding contests, offering discounts or coupons and posting photos of staff members.

Once you establish a personal connection, the bond will continue through social media.

519. After posting content, measure

Monitor which posts generate the most engagement and which ones get no or very little response. This is a great way to find out what works and what doesn't and then you can tweak your messaging or posts from there.

520. Follow the rule of thirds when it comes to posting information

That is, one third of your posts should be about your business, one third replying and engaging with others, and one third reposting or sharing what others are saying.

521. Vary your content

Every social media channel has a different audience, so don't post the exact same content to Facebook and Twitter.

522. Be clear about your goals for Facebook

Clarify what you want to achieve business-wise from it. Is it to open up another avenue to attract more clients? Get more traffic to your blog? Boost the numbers of people opting in to your newsletter?

523. Pick the best Page type for your purpose

- If you're setting up a Facebook Page for a brick and mortar business like a hairdressing salon or restaurant, choose Local Business or Place

- If you're creating a Page for a product brand, an online business, a freelance company or a website, choose Brand or Product

- If you're setting up a Page on behalf of a company or organisation, choose Company, Organization or Institution

524. Take care spelling your Facebook Page name

Once you have 100 fans, you can no longer edit the name of your Page so make sure you get it right the first time.

525. Choose a short, simple Facebook Page name

Long or descriptive Page names don't work as well as simple, short Page names.

526. Understand what it all means

When a Facebook user 'Likes' your Page, this means:

- A link to your Page will appear on the user's Info tab

- A notification that they've Liked your Page will appear on their profile (temporarily) under Recent Activity

- Your posts will now appear in their News Feed

When a user likes an update on your Page, this means:

- Other users can see that they have Liked the item. If enough people Like the update, their name will be replaced by a total count of Likes. This doesn't share the update in any way and is primarily a source of social proof

When a user Likes your content on another website (outside of Facebook) this means

- It will increase the number of people who are shown as liking the content, which adds social proof

- An update is posted to their Facebook profile saying that they liked the content. The update links to the content they liked

- An update is posted to their friends' News Feeds saying that they Liked the content, and linking to it

The most important of these actions is Liking your Page.

Once a user Likes your Page, they'll be subscribed to your updates forever, unless they Unlike your Page or close their account. This is a powerful way to keep the user engaged with your brand over the long-term.

The second most valuable form of a Like is a Like on your content.

This shares the content with the user's Facebook network and can drive new visitors to your website, blog or store.

The least valuable form of a Like is a Like on an update you've posted to your Page. This is useful for social proof, but little else. It's still a good thing to have, but there's no need to worry about this too much. Post good content and the Likes will follow.

527. A few active fans are better than lots of inactive fans

Aim for a large and engaged community. It's better to have active fans than a ton of inactive fans.

528. Offer discount codes and coupons to your fans

Many companies post discounts specifically for Facebook fans. This is a great way to make your fans feel special while giving exposure to your product and encouraging sales.

529. Engage with video.

Video can be a more intimate form of communication than writing. By talking to your fans 'face to face' through video, you can bring them closer to you. Video content on Facebook has another impressive benefit. If you upload video to Facebook, rather than linking over to YouTube or another video hosting service, your video will display a 'Like' button when viewed by someone who's not yet a fan of your Page. If they click that Like button, they'll become a fan. For this reason, it's often best to host your video content on Facebook directly.

530. Don't post and run

Don't just post something and then leave. You should be active in the comments on your own Facebook posts. One of the most helpful ways a fan can interact with your Facebook Page is by commenting. To encourage comments, answer direct questions, and thank people for their comments, even if they're not specifically looking for a response. Additionally, you can use comments to add persuasive weight, or extra information, to your posts.

To apply for a free implementation session **worth £495** where we show you how everything in this book can be done for you, go to **completedigitalmarketingsystem.com/121**

165

531. More is better

Because posts are naturally limited in length, and more comments means that your Page will spread further on Facebook, it's ideal to update your Page a number of times per day if possible. The next best thing is to update once a day, and the next best thing after that is to update a few times a week. How much time you commit depends on how important Facebook is to your business, and how much you enjoy creating Facebook content.

532. Create custom tabs

You can create and leverage custom tabs which are accessible via the 'Views & Apps' section of your Page. Think of these as landing pages within your Facebook page. You can use them as calls to action to feature anything from case studies to marketing offers to other promotions you're running.

533. Highlight your accomplishments

Facebook's page design supports 'Milestones,' which allow you to call attention to significant events in your business's history. Use the feature to highlight some of your biggest accomplishments, such as fan growth, award wins, product releases, major events, or other accolades. You can create a new (or past) milestone via the status update box, which will prompt you to input information about your milestone such as its name, location, date, story description and an image.

534. Offer fan-only content

One way to increase the number of people who like your page is to offer them incentives such as discount codes, bonus content or sneak peeks at upcoming events or products/services that are only visible to fans. To be able to access the content, they must first Like the Page. Your call to action button could say something like, "Click the Like button to become a fan and get an exclusive [detail what they'll get]."

535. Use Facebook Insights

Facebook Insights is Facebook's internal analytics tool that helps you measure and analyse your Facebook presence. The tool provides Facebook page administrators with analytics data about page visits and engagement and can help you understand which content is and isn't engaging to your fans. Access your page's Insights at http://www.facebook.com/insights or by clicking into the 'Admin Panel' on your page.

536. Offer incentives that will encourage visitors to become fans

What kind of incentives will encourage your Facebook Page visitors to become fans? Try these:

- Discount coupons

- Access to special events

- Secret information

- Free resources

- Exclusive content

537. Star or hide posts

Modify the items in your page's timeline to highlight certain posts more prominently than others. By hovering over individual stories, you can make them wider and more prominent on your page by clicking the star icon, or hide them from your timeline (or delete them entirely) by clicking on the pencil icon.

538. 37. Capture the interest of visitors with videos

Videos involve a longer commitment from your Facebook audience. But when it comes to having content variety on your page, a video can be a nice change of pace. Just be sure that when you do post a video, it's good enough to merit a visitor's time.

539. Know the key data to look at

- Facebook Insights gives you lots of data but there are three that are really important to look at in terms of how your content is performing on Facebook:

- Lifetime Total Likes

- Daily Friends of Fans

- Daily Page Consumption

These three figures will help you understand how your content is performing on Facebook. Lifetime Total Likes tells you exactly how many people like your page, Daily Friends of Fans tells you how many friends of those total likes can be reached – your true total reach – and Daily Page Consumption tells you the number of people (out of the possible number of people who could have been reached) that were actually reached.

Assess your content strategy using Facebook Insights on a consistent basis, whether that is daily, weekly, or monthly.

540. Grab attention with quotes or facts

Sometimes the easiest way to grab the attention from your audience is to simply post a statistic relevant to your industry or a quote from an influencer in your industry. This type of short-form content demands a very low commitment from the reader, making it easier for them to accept and act on the message via a Like, comment, or share.

541. Experiment with Interest Lists

'Interest Lists' are a feature that allows users to organise updates into separate topics from a collection of fan pages and/or public figures who have the subscribe button enabled on their profile.

Users can also subscribe to Interest Lists created by other people, as Facebook suggests popular lists and make it easy for users to discover lists created by their friends. Consider experimenting with

Interest Lists by creating lists in your industry; promoting the 'Add to Interest Lists' button on your Facebook page; creating content about industry news so your updates are the first to show up in any lists your business is apart of; and creating a must-subscribe, content-rich Facebook presence.

542. Consider advertising on Facebook

Facebook advertising works on a bidding model similar to Google ads. You bid on the price you are willing to pay to have your ad shown, and then you are charged in either one of two ways:

- Cost per click (CPC): you get charged when someone clicks on your ad.

- Cost per thousand (CPT): this method charges you per 1,000 people who see your advertisement.

Google advertising uses keywords in your Google searches to determine which ads to display. With Facebook ads, you bid on target demographics and keywords that appear in user profiles.

543. Set goals for your ad campaign

What do you want from your Facebook advertising campaign? If you are directing all traffic to your website, what does success look like? A newsletter sign-up? A product purchase? If you are sending all traffic to your Facebook Page, your conversions to 'Likes' are tracked in the stats.

Set up a formal campaign that outlines different types of ads to split test. Split testing involves changing one piece of the ad, such as the photo, and keeping the other elements the same to see which ad performs better. Rotate your ads frequently to keep them fresh.

544. Track leads generated from Facebook Campaigns

To understand the success of your overall Facebook marketing, and the efforts powered by the advertising campaigns, analyse three metrics:

- Unique Visits to Website: track the volume of overall traffic Facebook is sending your website

- Net New Leads (Contacts): track the number of new leads, also called contacts, which you're generating from your Facebook marketing and advertising efforts

- Customers Converted: over time, you'll want to assess the overall percentage of customers generated through your Facebook marketing

545. Keep your Facebook ads simple

The best performing ads on Facebook use clear, concise sentences and proper grammar.

546. Do use a call to action in your Facebook ad

Give your ad viewers a specific action to take such as 'Click to learn more!'

547. Pick a strong call to action

Your call to action must trigger a response in your viewers. Choose one of the following strong calls to action to use in your ads:

- Be the first to

- Click here to

- Sign up here

- Join now

- See it now

- Don't miss out

- Click to learn more

548. Use a relevant image in your Facebook ad

If you're promoting something other than your Facebook Page, upload a relevant image. The maximum image size is 110px wide by

80px tall. If you're selling a product, for example, use a good image of the product. If you're selling a service, your logo may work well. Just make sure that whatever image you choose is something that will appeal to your target market.

549. Narrow your focus for your Facebook ad

Unless you have a huge budget for your Facebook ad, you need to narrow your target audience. Broad targeting will cost you dearly and waste your efforts. Your aim should be to get a low ratio of views to clicks so that you get more returns for your advertising budget. To achieve that, you need to ensure your ad is only seen by the people who are most likely to click on it.

550. If you're a local business, choose a city level target

Don't waste your advertising budget by targeting the entire country if you're a local business. Instead, choose 'City' as your location target.

551. Run small tests of your Facebook ad

Before committing to a large advertising campaign, conduct small tests first. Try a few variations of your ad to determine which one gets the best response.

552. Don't use a group to market your business

Groups are solely intended for Facebook users to connect with each other around common interests and goals – not a single brand – which is why it's a big mistake to try to use it as an advertising / sales opportunity.

553. Don't post with shortened URLs

BuddyMedia, a salesforce.com company, conducted a study that revealed that full-length URLs get three times as many clicks as shortened URLs. In other words, using shortened URLs on Facebook actually has a negative impact on your ability to create awareness about your business. Rather than using shortened URLs, post content directly on Facebook, or use a third-party tool like Post Planner (www.postplanner.com), which is made specifically for Facebook marketers to schedule and post various types of content to a Facebook Page.

554. Don't be pushy

Selling too much is probably the most common mistake by Facebook marketers. Facebook users won't want to be confronted by a hard sales pitch. They don't tend to care too much about products or services but do care about things related to those products or services.

555. Don't sell too little

Don't be afraid to sell. Facebook users love to talk about the things they care about, but they also love a good deal!

556. Don't post long updates

One study by BuddyMedia found that status updates of less than 80 characters received a 27% higher reaction than longer updates. If you make the updates too long, there's a strong chance that many people won't bother reading them. Short updates such as questions and short polls get a higher reaction simply because the barrier to participation is very low.

557. Don't ignore comments

If people make the effort to leave a comment or reply within a thread on your Facebook Page, they want to know that you're paying attention. Pages that consistently ignore posts by fans aren't as successful as Pages that participate in comment threads. Fans are less likely to return if they don't feel noticed or acknowledged. The other reason why you should respond to posts from fans is that Facebook sends that person a notification, bringing him or her back to your Page. So, in addition to showing fans that they are heard, you also get them to continue posting on your Page.

558. Don't be afraid to ignore people

You don't have to respond to every comment or post that you receive (unless they're criticisms of your company and/or content: in which case, respond super fast!). Sometimes fans can overuse the various communication features in Facebook. Make a point of always welcoming new fans and responding to comments and posts on your timeline within 12 hours, but know when to let the conversation rest. For example, if the same fan leaves several comments on a single post, replying once should be enough.

559. Deal with angry, negative comments fast

If someone posts a negative comment, respond quickly to diminish the negative impact it could have on your business. Facebook is a public network so anyone can post a comment. Be polite at all times, no matter how much you might want to really 'let rip'.

560. The best ways to deal with an irate fan

Find and establish common ground. Consider the other person's point of view and see if you can find something to agree with. Correct any factual information tactfully and pleasantly. Don't try to score points – you'll just look bad. Say if you don't know the solution to a particular problem. Don't bluff or resort to meaningless jargon to squirm your way out of a problem. Just let the person know you'll get the correct information. Let the person know how long that might take. Take the conversation offline if possible.

561. Appreciate and recognise your fans

If you want to stand apart from the crowd on Facebook, make a concerted effort to recognise and appreciate your Facebook fans.

562. Measure and monitor

What you're measuring on Facebook is the response from your efforts. What topics get people excited? Which fan acquisition strategies are working best? When fans click to your website, how many of them end up as customers? If you can't answer these questions, you'll never know whether you're using Facebook effectively. In today's economy, you can't afford to wing it. Think about measuring your Facebook efforts as a compass that tells you how far away you are from your destination, when you have arrived, and how to change direction, if needed.

563. Create engaging content

Post a variety of content, from photos and status updates, to videos, events, and polls. Ask your audience questions and have them post their answers in the comments section of your post. Not only does this engage your current fans, it will make the post visible in the news feeds of your fans, thus increasing your reach to their friends who may not yet know about you.

564. Try out Facebook Groups

Groups on Facebook are slightly different than business pages. In some cases, it makes sense for a business to create a group as well. The main difference between a business page and a group is that pages represent a brand, while a group is a place for a community of people to discuss common interests. A group is essentially a page that is used as a chat room for a specific group of people. In a group, members can post all kinds of content just like on personal timelines and business pages.

565. Avoid the temptation to sell, sell, sell

Don't oversell or undersell. It's not easy to get the right balance but it's important to try nonetheless. You won't make any friends by indulging in a never-ending sales pitch but, at the same time, you should highlight your products and services. Use the 80-20 rule for sales messages vs. content/connection posts. So if you decide to post five times a week, one of the posts should be a sales message and the other four posts should be other helpful content.

566. Use birthday targeting

Many users on Facebook share their birthdays. Get their attention by sending them a special birthday offer.

567. Target interests and hobbies

Target by interests and hobbies that describe your best brand fans. For example, if you sell financial services, look for fans of well-known financial advisors or readers of investment newspapers/magazines.

568. Use the best ad types to drive offsite sales and leads

There are a number of ad units that can be used in fulfilling direct response advertising objectives to drive sales and leads. Those are:

- External website ads: perfect for ensuring all your clicks are directed towards your website

- Offer ads: Facebook offer ads provide a great way to incentivise and track new customers by providing an offer. When a user claims the offer, it creates a story that can be published on their friends' New Feeds, allowing your advertising to reach new targets.

- Page posts: Advertisers can include links in their Page posts that direct users to external websites. This gives advertisers the ability to utilise users' News Feeds with rich content while still channelling traffic to their external websites.

569. Provide relevant contact details to your Facebook business page

Add enough contact details to your header. Do include your URL and email details. If you're a local company, include your address and phone numbers.

570. Use visually stimulating images

Facebook users like images. Take advantage of this by using captivating and stimulating images when and where possible. Images are the most common thread to go viral on Facebook. They're therefore more likely to generate shares, likes and comments, which will expose your brand to a wider audience.

571. Optimise your Facebook Page for mobile users

Check out what your users see on your Page by checking out your Facebook Page on your own mobile device. (Look at Public view not Admin view.)

Highlight your best content with a pinned post, since mobile viewers won't see your complete timeline.

Make sure your posts, offers and ads feature colourful, interesting images since photos are the best-performing post types on Facebook.

572. If you have a local business, encourage your customers to check in on Facebook at your location.

Mobile searchers tend to make local buying decisions (e.g., where to eat, where to shop, etc.). Recommendations and check-ins from mobile users' friends appear first on their mobile devices, making it a fantastic tool for word-of-mouth marketing.

573. Paid Ads improve reach

According to the 2013 Social Rich Media Benchmark Report (ShopIgniter), promoting your Facebook posts with a paid ad increases organic and viral reach significantly but reduces click-throughs. This is true for all post types (video, offers, photos, links and questions) except status updates. In the case of status updates, unpaid posts have a much higher reach than paid posts. Paid ads make a big difference on Facebook–at least in terms of reach and impressions.

Paid ads are used for promotional content, which by default draws less engagement than non-promotional content. If you're more interested in driving brand awareness or increasing your customer base, then by all means use paid ads because of their viral nature. But if you're trying to build your email list (you'll need people to click through to a landing page), then paying to promote the post might be a waste of cash, according to the research. And don't forget, whenever you want people to click, give them lots of images!

574. Negative feedback hurts conversion

Research from ShopIgniter shows that negative feedback (including Hide Post, Hide All Posts, Report as Spam, Unlike Page) hurts conversions the more you add paid media to your posts. For most post types except links, negative feedback increases when paid ads are used.

575. Discover what images your audience likes best

Although photos are popular on Facebook, not all photos are created equal. As a marketer, find out exactly what your audience's preferences are by posting photos they will enjoy, like and share. If you're not sure, do some A/B split tests with various images to find out.

576. Facebook hashtags are not popular

Hashtags are very popular on Twitter but research by EdgeRank Check reveals that Facebook posts with hashtags are less likely to go viral and make people less likely to engage with the content. If you want your fans and their friends to share your Facebook posts, either avoid using hashtags or conduct your own tests to see whether they help or hurt your brand.

577. Mention your fans by name in the comments on your Facebook posts

This is one of the best ways to give a personal touch to your brand's Facebook presence. In some cases you'll be able to use an @ sign and tag a user in your comments to them, in other cases you'll just have to type out their name. Either way, this gives a personal feeling that social media is all about, connecting with your advocates one on one.

578. Measure successful engagement per post

Aim to get 1% of your audience to interact with each post that is shared on your Page. Just take your existing audience size, divide it by 100 and the result will be the number of people who should be engaging with your post via shares, comments and likes.

579. Improve the SEO of your Facebook Page

Set three keyword rich sub-categories for your Place Page. Go to Edit Page, then Basic Information and then define these sub-categories keeping Facebook search and the search engines in mind.

580. Enable users to tag your Facebook Page in their photos

This will help organically grow your audience and impressions. Go to Edit Page, then Manage Permissions and be sure to check off the box that says People can add tags to photos by [Your Page Name].

581. Incorporate photos in line with your other posting strategies

This will help you to get higher visibility in the newsfeed. Photos have a higher weight with Facebook's EdgeRank (plus people love them), so use them when you can with other strategies to help get your content get more traction.

582. Do use Facebook Questions

Add some variety to the content you share and poll your audience to see what aspects of your brand they really enjoy.

583. Use pounds off rather than percent for Facebook offers

A study by BuddyMedia found money off offers generated twice the engagement of those that detailed "% off" for the retail industry on Facebook. Test your market to gauge what offer works best.

584. Use fill in the blanks style posts

Encourage more people to interact with a fill in the blank style post.

585. Know the difference between Google and Facebook ads

When you write an ad for Google, you target people with keywords. That way, you know your ad shows up for people searching for the service or product you provide. In that respect, Google ads are about what people want.

Facebook is different. People don't use Facebook to find solutions to problems. They go there to catch up with friends. Facebook is about people, and as such, Facebook ads target particular groups of people. Facebook ads are about who you want to engage with.

So think about the type of people who need/want your products or services. If you don't already know, research to find out:

- Where they live

- Their age

- Their interests

- Their industry/market

- Their relationship status

Facebook lets you target all of these aspects in ads. You can select everything from activities your target audience is interested in (from food to gardening to literature) to their interests (from politics to wine tasting, etc.), to the films, movies and sports they like.

586. Sharpen your focus

The tighter the focus of your ad, the better it will perform. However, don't get so targeted that your ad is aimed at a handful of people (unless you're selling Lear jets, in which case a handful of buyers may be all the market you need!)

587. Use ads to capture your different targets

You may discover your clients' interests and demographics fall into several distinct groups. If this is the case, consider running a separate ad campaign for each group.

588. Brainstorm lots of ad ideas

You probably won't come up with the best ad on your first attempt. So write lots down. Narrow the list until you've got at least 20 ad ideas. Each one can be up to 90 characters long. However, shorter can be better, so don't feel obliged to fill your character allocation.

589. Pick your focus

Give your ad a specific focus. People want to know exactly what they'll get out of liking your ad or engaging with your company. For example, promoting your information guide will draw more engagement than promoting your business in general. You can focus on a specific service or product. To make your ad even more powerful, also focus on the benefits of working with you.

590. Do include your company name in your ad

Ads that include the name of the company they're promoting perform better than those that don't. Tweak your copy to include the name of your business.

591. Tell users what to do

Tell users what to do. Conclude your ad with a call to action. Use a phrase such as "Click to like".

592. Use a selection of ads for each campaign

Facebook ads have a short shelf life. If you're targeting well, the same people will keep seeing your ad over and over again, so it will get old fast. Usually, interest in ads drops off after three to five days. If you're planning a campaign that lasts longer than three to five days, you'll need to mix things up to maintain interest, so it's a good idea to prepare a series of ads.

593. Use coloured borders on your ad

Coloured borders grab attention, especially if the colour contrasts with Facebook's own colour scheme.

594. Make sure the ad image reflects your company brand

Only use an image that reinforces the message and your brand's personality.

595. Monitor and tweak your ads

Check in daily to see how your campaign is going. The more you're willing to tweak and try out different ideas for your copy and images, the better your results will be. In other words, see what works, and do more of it!

596. Create a killer headline

Write what you want to communicate in as long a sentence as necessary, without worrying about style, vernacular, or length. This is a way to get you thinking about what your headline needs to say.

Once you've clarified what the headline needs to say, start playing with words. You have a 25-character limit so finding the right words is crucial. Obviously, with the restrictions on length, you need to look for short words that convey precisely what you want to say. Brainstorm until you've got a selection of possible headlines.

Here are some possibilities to consider:

- Ask a question
- Ask a question but omit the question mark (which saves space)
- Tout the benefits
- Focus on a negative outcome
- Call out to the demographic segment you're targeting (for example, 'Attention Dentists!')

597. Craft your ad message carefully

The main part of your ad (the body text) can only be 90 characters long. That's why every word you use is critical. To craft the best message, consider the keywords you want to feature in the ad. Then consider the benefits of your offer to visitors. What problem will it solve for them? Sometimes starting your message with a question can really engage your visitor and convince him or her that you understand the problem. Follow the question by identifying the benefit that will solve the problem.

598. Don't assume readers will know what to do

Your ad must finish with a strong call to action. This may seem obvious but it's surprising how many experienced marketers forget to include a strong call to action at the end of a message. Don't ever assume your reader will take the action you want him or her to take. You must tell them what to do. Use a command such as, "Click to access your free report" or "Click to get a free quote".

599. Make sure your landing page matches the call to action in the advert

The landing page or web page you send readers to from your Facebook ad must match the call to action in your ad. For example, if your ad asks readers to sign up for your newsletter, the landing page or web page must feature a sign-up box for your newsletter. Make it easy for your readers to take the desired action. If the page is in any way confusing or inconvenient for your readers, they will leave without taking the desired action.

600. Don't accept Facebook's suggest an ad link

Facebook can suggest an ad link for you while you're creating your ad for an external site but it's probably better not to accept it. Why? The suggested ad copy is pulled from the information in your website description, which may be too general. Furthermore, the picture placed in the suggested ad could be from anywhere on your website and may not be relevant to the specific ad.

Your ad will be more effective if you craft your own message – with your own title and text, and an appropriate picture. You can use the suggested ad tool to pull in a logo quickly; then you can modify the ad as necessary.

601. Make your ad eye-catching with the right image

Images make your ad more eye catching, and Facebook now requires them anyway. An image can be a logo, photo, or icon and should relate to the title and body text of the ad. The photo should be clear and not too "busy": it'll only be 100 pixels wide and 72 pixels tall.

Chapter 7
Landing Pages That Convert

In a Nutshell

To minimise the chances of your prospects clicking away from your website never to return and maximise the results of your online promotions, you need to use a landing page.

A landing page is a specially designed page and the first one a visitor will see after clicking on or entering a specific link or web address. When they click on an online advertisement (a pay per click advertisement or a banner ad, an email link, or the result of a web search), they will be directed to a landing page.

A properly designed landing page will give your prospects the information they are looking for and will increase your chances of converting them. A poorly developed landing page can undermine an otherwise successful promotional campaign.

For this reason, creating the right landing page is crucial to any online ad campaign.

The landing page's effectiveness is measured by its conversion rate, meaning how often people who visit the page do whatever it is you want them to do

The following tips are designed to ensure your landing pages meet your objectives and get the highest number of visitors to take the desired action.

602. Define exactly what you want your visitors to do

This is the goal, or conversion objective, of your landing page and should completely drive the development of the page.

What action do you want visitors to take on your landing page? Common landing page objectives include:

- Boost sales

- Create/update customer information base

- Get subscribers

Whatever it is you want visitors to do, it is vital that your landing page be clear, easy to read, and focused on the conversion objective.

603. Don't send people to your homepage

Your homepage contains too many competing messages. You need to provide a place that has one goal, one message, and one action. In other words, a landing page.

604. Provide a consistent experience for users

From ad through landing page and onto the destination site, design, messaging and tone should be consistent with the expectations your user had at the time they clicked the link/banner.

605. Get to the point – fast

Don't waste your visitors' time: give them what they've come for immediately.

606. Focus your visitors' attention with a clear and concise headline

Make the headline clear, easily noticeable, and in a relevant position on the page.

607. User and traffic segmentation

If you have multiple user types, create a landing page for each segment and drive traffic via separate sources. This will enable you to measure your most effective market segmentation. It will also mean that you can design each separate landing page according to the traffic source.

608. Devote adequate resources to each component of your landing page programme

A successful landing page programme has four components:

- Research
- Design
- Copy
- Testing and Modification

It is important to devote adequate resources to each component. If you fail to properly research your audience, then the greatest design will never save the campaign. Similarly, a prospect might click away from copy that is too long or too short, regardless of how much research went into its development.

609. Know your customer

Converting visitors to customers or leads is the entire focus of your landing page and knowing as much as possible about them is the foundation of the page.

- Who is the potential customer you want to attract to your page?
- What will bring that customer to your site, and keep them there?
- What matters most to them?
- How much money are they willing to spend?
- How much information will they give?

The answers to these questions will help you to provide the details that will be critical to your landing page's success. Focus your attention on knowing your customers and keeping them in mind as you create your landing page – if you do this it will make them feel you are speaking directly to them and that you understand their needs.

610. Keep the landing page focused on a single product or message

Having several calls to action lined up next to each other focused on multiple goals and objectives will create friction (fear, doubt, and uncertainty) and reduce conversion.

611. Give them what they are looking for

You need to make sure that customers arrive at the exact information they expect. That is why it is important that your promotions lead visitors to relevant landing pages, and not the homepage of your website. You cannot risk losing your customer's focus by forcing them to search for the information they need from your homepage.

612. Remove distractions

The focus of your design is conversion, so anything that diverts your visitor from that is detrimental to your goal. If visitors to your landing page are distracted, they may lose focus and not take the desired action. There is one and only one topic of interest on your landing page, and anything else should be removed. Get rid of any information, pictures, or items that may sidetrack your visitor.

613. Keep the design simple

Don't crowd your landing page – keep it simple. Get rid of the navigation bar (so that visitors aren't tempted to go wandering off before taking the desired action).

614. Make the conversion as easy as possible

The less time users must spend on your conversion activity, the less time they have to change their mind. So if you have an ecommerce site, don't force your landing page visitors to register before placing an order. And if you have a lead generation website, make your online information form simple. Limit the amount of fields your visitor is required to fill out. For example, it helps to have the input cursor jump to the next field in the form on its own. If possible, have the fields pre-populate if possible. Focus on capturing only the absolutely essential information.

615. Never put a 'clear form' button next to the 'submit' button

If a visitor accidentally presses 'clear form' and loses all the information they've just entered, they're likely to be so annoyed they leave without re-entering the information.

616. Resist the temptation to use the latest web graphic effects

Using too much technology will distract visitors, and your message may be lost. The focus of your page needs to be completely on getting visitors to perform the desired action. Get rid of any flash animation – some companies have improved their conversion rates by between 20% and 60% by simply removing flash from landing pages.

617. Be sure that your landing page takes five seconds or less to load

Visitors don't have the patience to wait more than five seconds for a page to load.

618. Make sure your privacy policy is easy to understand and easy to locate

This will reassure your prospective clients that their privacy is important to you and will be well protected. Let them know that you have taken the time to create safeguards for their information. Place a link to your privacy policy, an icon that shows precautions have been taken or a simple statement such as "Your privacy is important to us", in close proximity to the fields where you want customers to enter personal information.

619. Remove the perceived risk for your prospective clients or customers

Reassure visitors that signing up for your product or service is risk-free. Offer your customers a warranty for products, or a trial period for services. Suggest free consultations for new clients to get a feel for your services without spending any money.

620. Cut anxiety by offering testimonials

Feature customer testimonials on your landing page. This will lower the fear, anxiety and doubt your prospective customers or clients have about dealing with you. Make sure the testimonials are concise and relevant to the subject of the landing page.

User testimonials should speak of the benefits of your products or services and be relevant to your target audience.

621. Only use testimonials that feature some form of identification

Don't use testimonials that only have people's initials underneath them or worse, no identifying features. They will look fake. That will destroy your credibility in an instant. When the testimonial includes a client's full name, place of residence, or even photo of the user, it becomes more credible. All your testimonials must be genuine, descriptive, brief, and convincing.

622. Include evidence of media coverage and associations with credible organisations

You can allay your visitors' fears, uncertainties, and doubts by showing positive media coverage, industry certifications, awards, memberships, and standard compliances.

623. Be aware of 'the fold'

The fold is the point on a web page when scrolling is required to view the additional content. If visitors have to scroll to get all the information from your landing page, especially the call to action, you may lose them. Therefore, it is important to know where the fold will fall. Since different browsers, and different screen resolutions, will place the fold at different points on your page, you need to design your page for the lowest common denominator – a screen resolution of 800 x 600. Your page design needs to be a little smaller to account for the title, menu bars, and frames of common browsers. This means the size of your page should be no more than 750 x 500.

624. Place the call to action above the fold

Many of your visitors will not scroll, regardless of how important the information is below the fold. For that reason, it's vital that you place the call to action above the fold to capture the attention of those non-scrollers.

625. If your page is long, use more than one call to action

Depending on the length of your page, you may need to place your call to action in more than one position. Use one call to action for every 'screen', or about every 400 to 500 lines of vertical resolution.

626. Don't have a break in your text on or near the fold

Web browsers automatically add scroll bars to longer pages, but users don't always notice them. Try to not have a distinct break in your copy at or near the fold, or your reader may not know to scroll down.

627. Keep the most important items centred in your visitor's line of sight

Place the key elements (graphics, text, etc.) in the centre of the viewer's line of sight. This should be the focal point of the page. Don't allow items on the sidebars to take attention away from this focus. Your message should be extremely conspicuous so that readers who scan the webpage will get your message.

628. Use big, bold, colourful text and images for key elements

A quick glance at your landing page should be enough for someone to know what you are offering. For that to happen, your key text and images should really stand out on the page.

629. Use the same graphics and colours on the page as in your advert

Use the same graphics and colours that were used in any other promotional creative material (ads, banners, etc.) relating to your page. Changing the colour scheme which your visitor has become acquainted with can cause confusion and lead the visitor to click away.

630. Don't let supporting graphics overpower your main image

If you use supporting graphic elements (such as a chart or graph) to help convey your message make sure that they don't overpower other elements and become the focus of your page. This could distract the viewer from continuing on the path to conversion.

631. Lead the users' eyes along the page towards the call to action

The flow of your page should naturally lead to a conversion exit. Web page viewers tend to look at a page starting from the top left and moving to the bottom right. The design of your page should follow this flow.

632. Make sure your landing page is easy to read

Choose font styles and colours carefully. Your page should use a familiar font and style. The page should be organised, easy to follow, and well spread out.

633. Check often that all links, buttons, and forms are working

A conversion is impossible if your potential customer clicks on "Order" and nothing happens. Moreover, this may change their mind about your product or offer for good. Technical glitches happen but by checking links, forms and buttons often, you will become aware of problems sooner.

To apply for a free implementation session **worth £495** where we show you how everything in this book can be done for you, go to **completedigitalmarketingsystem.com/121**

634. Prevent compatibility issues

Be sure your landing page works with all browsers and operating systems most commonly used by your users (look at your analytic data for stats).

635. Don't lose visitors

If you want conversions, you must direct visitors on what to do, and the order in which to do it. Your landing page should be easy to navigate, with clear links and buttons to keep users on course. Buttons and links should be clearly visible with a quick glance around the page. Underlining and using colour in your links will make them easier to identify. Additionally, buttons and links should lead users through the page and make the conversion process clear and simple.

636. Use the right image

A carefully chosen and well positioned image should be a major element of your landing page design. When scanning a web page, visitors will most often look at the image first. It can make the difference between whether or not your visitor stays.

The important criterion for choosing an image is relevance to the product or service that is being promoted. Do place it above the fold.

637. Limit the number of images

Multiple images will cause the visitor to lose focus. You want the visitor to look at a single image that will get them to move on to the next element in your page design.

If visitors start looking at more than one image, the progression towards conversion is often interrupted, resulting in a higher chance of them leaving without taking any action.

638. Make the call to action obvious and clear on your page

Along with the headline, image and body copy, the call to action should be distinct and easily identifiable. Your call to action is the primary conversion goal of a visitor to your landing page. Using a quick tag line within your call to action, succinctly indicating what action is expected, will help it stand out. Examples of common actions that need to be called out are: purchasing a product, subscribing to a newsletter, calling you on the phone, downloading an ebook or whitepaper, watching a demo or requesting information. If you're offering a free book then make the button say 'Get your free book' and not 'Go', 'Submit' or 'Subscribe'.

639. Test the colour of your call to action button

Changing the colour on a call to action button can translate into a 5% or 10% increase in conversion rates for a particular page. If you do have multiple buttons on the page, then make sure that the call to action button for the primary purpose of the page stands out from the rest of the buttons.

640. Experiment with different wording on your call to action

Try different wording on your call to action to see which one works better for your visitors.

641. Don't use the word 'submit' in your call to action

The standard wording of "Submit" on a call to action will generally have a negative impact on your conversion rates.

642. Don't place your call to action too close to other key elements

Having the call to action immediately below the headline, immediately beside your image or in the middle of your body copy will reduce its visibility and the effectiveness of the other elements. Since the call to action is the main objective of any landing page, it should have its own space.

643. Place your logo where it will be seen

Given the scanning habits of viewers, the top left corner of your page will generally be your prospect's starting point which makes it a good place for your logo. It will reinforce a basic element of your message, who you are. Even if they view your image first, it is easy for them to glance up before moving on.

644. Separate your testimonials from the main copy

Highlight the testimonial by using a different font colour or italics.

645. Use sans serif fonts for readability

Sans serif fonts are easier to read, especially at the smaller sizes that you would use for your body copy. What's more, serif fonts don't display as well on computer monitors. Exceptions might be the font used for testimonial copy or text that can be displayed at a larger font size. Use a point size of at least 10 since small type is more difficult to read which means your readers will be less likely to continue on the page.

Don't reduce the size of your font to get more information above the fold.

646. Balance the elements on your landing page with space

Use space between elements. That will allow your visitor to observe and absorb it without too many distractions by adjacent elements. Even the spacing you use needs to be balanced. A large open space on your screen can be a place for your visitor to become lost, lose focus, and click away.

647. Use short length copy for giveaways or free offers

Generally, it's best to use short length copy for giveaways or free offers. If visitors want what you are offering, they don't want to read too much, they just want the freebie. Since this is a general rule, test your market to see what works best.

648. Long copy works better if you are selling expensive items

Visitors want to know as much as they can about something before they part with their hard-earned money so want lots of information.

Having said that, you should test your market to find out what length copy works best.

649. Maintain visitors' interest with succinct copy

Online visitors read less copy on a web page than they would in a brochure or other printed material. Maintain their interest, by making your copy brief and to the point. Irrelevant information, clichés, and hyperbole will increase abandonments.

650. Keep paragraphs brief, no matter the length of your copy

Longer paragraphs can be intimidating. With a short paragraph, the decision to continue reading is made easier. Generally, paragraphs should be no more than two or three sentences, depending on the length of each sentence.

651. Use keywords

Not everyone will come to your landing through banner ads or links you have set up. Many will have entered a word or phrase – keywords – in a search engine and clicked on the resulting organic or paid links that appealed to them. It is important to have your page copy match that of the link or ad used by the customer. You don't want visitors thinking they're in the wrong place because your page copy is different from the copy on the link they used.

652. Put important information where it will be seen

Most visitors will simply scan your copy, regardless of how precise and appropriate it is. Scanners are more likely to read and remember the first and last sentence or two of copy and the first and last points in a list. So, be sure to position your most important information where it will have the best chance of being read and recalled.

653. Make your headline stand out on the page

Your headline should stand out so use a larger font size, different colours, or a combination of both.

654. Use plain language

Using easy to understand language will mean that you will get your message across in the quickest way possible and more of your visitors will understand your message.

655. Have only one primary conversion goal for your landing page

You can have multiple conversion objectives for your site, but you should only have one primary conversion goal for the landing page. If you have multiple goals on a single landing page, you will lose focus of your main objective (conversion). When you lose focus, your conversion rate will drop.

656. Every element should support your value proposition

Value proposition is a statement that summarises why a prospect should buy your product or service. Every element on the landing page should either state the value proposition or support it. So images, copy, or incentives must point to the value proposition.

657. Use white space effectively

Too much white space can impact confidence negatively, whereas too little can create a clutter effect. You need to maintain a balance with white space making items clear and easy to navigate through.

658. Be aware of factors that cause anxiety in visitors

If something about the company, the product, or the site gives a user any doubt to continue, the visitor will leave the site quickly. Those factors include:

- An inability to locate the call to action

- Long forms with too many unnecessary fields

- Image load up time

- Browser compatibility

- Difficulty finding out what the site offers

- Limited images displaying product

- Poor headline

- Lack of continuity

As long as you are aware of the factors that may create anxiety and get in the way of the conversion process, you can deal with them.

659. You need at least one image on your landing page

An image on your landing page will help to grab visitors' attention and convey information much faster than a couple of paragraphs of text will. You have to be strategic with your choice of image however. For the image to be effective, it has to be relevant to what you're selling or promoting.

660. Remove the navigation bar

Your landing page visitors don't need the full-scale website experience so remove your navigation bar along with all the other distractions. Each navigation option you provide dilutes their attention.

661. Make your key point stand out

Don't bury the most important part of your message halfway down the page. Make it the first thing your visitors read.

662. People react to different content so give them plenty of opportunities to take action

A few of your landing page visitors will be so ready to buy that they'll pounce on the call to action button right at the top. Others will take longer to convince: they may be two thirds of the way through before they believe what you are saying. If there is a button right there, you may find them more likely to convert. And there will be a few who will read every single word on the entire page before they're ready to hit the call to action button so make sure you have one at the bottom of the page.

663. The elements on your landing page must be congruent

All the design and copy on your web page (including the layout, the colour of the background and text and call to action buttons) should support your core value proposition. Check it. If it's not congruent, rewrite or redesign the page.

664. Experiment with video

Test what impact a video has on your landing page.

665. Provide extra value on your confirmation or thank you page

If you're asking your visitors for personal data on your landing page (such as an email address for lead capture), take it one step further, and give them a bonus on the thank you page. This could just be something useful such as a link to related content on your site, or it could be an extra free report.

666. Provide a phone number

Having a phone number on your landing page shows visitors your company is legitimate and that there are people who they can contact if anything goes wrong. It can also be a good fall back for people who aren't comfortable with online transactions, but who like your offer.

667. Let people try before they sign up

If you are giving something away for free, but asking for personal details in exchange, offer something that really is for free in advance, such as a small portion of the materials you are providing (a chapter 1 preview, etc.). This piques interest and lets people know you're not going to send them something worthless in exchange for their personal information. People like the try-before-you-buy option.

668. If you make claims in your ads, verify them on your landing page

If you make any kind of claim ('UK's leading dental surgeon', for example) in your ad or banner, make sure you back up that claim on your landing page with third party endorsements or other credible sources. If your claim isn't true, it's better to leave it out.

669. Use endorsements

If you have affiliations with well known people or businesses, use their endorsements to build credibility.

670. Don't ask people for information you don't really need

Don't put people through the third degree on your landing page, asking for unnecessary details. You'll scare them off. Just ask for the information you really need. You can always find a way to get more information from them later.

671. Perform split tests on your testimonials

To measure the effect testimonials have on your landing page conversion rate, consider running an A/B split test (where one version of your landing page is compared with an almost identical page except for one key element). You could run tests to compare the following things:

- With and without testimonials

- With and without photos

- With short or full quotes

- With few or many testimonials

If you find that less testimonials work better, try using only one. Test a variety of testimonials in turn to see which people respond best to.

672. Use a professional to design your landing page

Don't be cheap: hire a professional to design your landing page for you. Yes, you could probably buy a programme to do it yourself or even find a free landing page template somewhere online. You could but the result will probably look rubbish. It's the equivalent of wearing home-made shoes to a business meeting. Creative, possibly. Professional, no.

673. Don't exaggerate

People aren't fools. They will come to your landing page with plenty of doubts about the veracity of your claims. Go too far with the hyperbole and they're likely to vanish.

674. If your strategic alliance or joint venture partner is sending traffic, use co-branding

If your strategic alliance or joint venture partner is sending visitors to your landing page, use a co-branded landing page to enhance the ad message momentum and improve your conversion rate. It will provide the visitor with the confidence that their intended goal is being maintained.

a. Include your partner's logo on the landing page alongside your own, to show that you have an established relationship

b. Repeat the offer. Show that clicking through to your landing page didn't cause the promise to be forgotten.

675. Provide a valuable resource to gain inbound links

If you give away something (a white paper, a special report, information guide or book, for example) that contains excellent content you are more likely to attract inbound links.

676. Lower your AdWords costs

The closer the content on your landing page can match the copy and link title from your AdWords campaigns, the more relevancy (and quality score) Google attributes to your intentions which results in a lower cost for your chosen Pay Per Click keywords.

677. Competitive analysis

Check out what your competitors are doing. This will give you inspiration for your own campaign, or if you are trying to innovate and differentiate, you will be in a position to move away from the competition.

To apply for a free implementation session **worth £495** where we show you how everything in this book can be done for you, go to **completedigitalmarketingsystem.com/121**

199

678. Analyse each campaign

After each landing page campaign, analyse what worked and what didn't. Record the results. Use the information (lessons learnt, etc.) in your future campaign.

679. Test the primary graphic image or photography

Most campaigns are intended for a specific segment or user demographic. As such, it's a good idea to try different images that provide varied emotional responses.

680. Test the main message

Write variations on your main message and run tests on each. Also try varying the size and colour of the text.

681. Test your call to action

Try varying the message in your main call to action. Ensure it's an accurate description of what the user will get when they act on it to avoid trust and annoyance issues.

682. Keep fields to a minimum

For lead capture and other form usage, minimise the number of fields in your forms.

If the design of lead generation forms is a source of internal conflict in your organisation, do the following to resolve the issue:

- Prioritise the fields in the lead capture form

- Set up a split test to see which fields perform better

- Analyse the results and choose the best fields to include in the lead generation form

683. Don't rest on your laurels

Test new ideas immediately. The more information you glean the better your landing pages will become. Don't stop at the first A/B test. Brainstorm areas of the page that should be tested.

684. Know the value of a conversion when planning your campaign budget

How much revenue do you make each time a conversion takes place on a landing page is important when coming up with a budget for a campaign. In the simple case of a sales landing page, that number usually is the average order size you receive from a conversion.

Total revenue from orders divided by the total number of orders equals your average order size. For example, if your landing page generates £1,000 of revenue from 25 orders then your average order size is £40.

However a conversion on a lead generation landing page doesn't mean an actual final sale. For this kind of landing pages, you need to evaluate what percentage of prospects who convert on the landing page are actually becoming clients or customers.

The number of final conversions divided by the number of landing page conversions multiplied by your average order size will give you the value of conversion for lead generation

685. Creating the perfect headline is critical

Your landing page's headline could make the difference between conversion and abandonment or bounce The fact that someone has arrived at your page means that they have an interest in your ad or have searched for your products or services. Your headline needs to affirm this interest and encourage further investigation.

686. Use directional cues to draw attention to the lead generation form

If your main goal is to have someone complete a form, then visually direct them to it so they know what they are supposed to do.

687. Use oversized buttons

Don't be afraid to use big buttons that really stand out. They don't need to be grey or be the same height as a standard text field.

688. Make form labels and field text easy to read

Use a large enough font that anyone can read your sign-up form easily.

689. Make it clear why filling out the form will be beneficial

The benefits and reward of filling out the form should be very clear. Position them in context with the form so that people are constantly reminded why they are bothering to fill out the form.

690. Reduce the available options

If you have only one message and action, you should be able to look at the page and have your eye immediately drawn to the action area. Don't place extraneous offers or navigation on the page that could draw the user into doing something else. In the case where you have several choices, there is still a single goal (choose a package), so ensure that each action area is consistent and they are grouped in a region that can be considered the action area.

691. Don't let visitors down

Deliver what you promise. If you can't, cancel the campaign. It's better to do that than risking untold damage to your company's reputation as a result of letting visitors down and not giving them what you'd promised.

692. Offer an alternative for nervous visitors

Not all customers are ready to engage right away and might need some supporting information to ease their worries or answer their questions. If you are asking someone to buy something, a sensible secondary call to action would be to offer a downloadable report.

This keeps them in your realm of influence (as opposed to leaving to do research elsewhere) and builds confidence. Ensure that the safety net call to action doesn't compete in size and visual dominance – often a simple text link is adequate, beneath the main big action button. If you are asking someone to purchase online, offering a phone number for phone orders can make a potential customer more likely to convert if that's their preferred contact method.

693. Use an appropriate message for your audience

Be sensitive to the market you're targeting and use appropriate language.

694. If video plays automatically, offer a 'mute' button

If your landing page features a video that plays automatically provide the facility to control the volume, including a prominent mute button. If someone is viewing your page during a quiet time or at the office, sudden sounds can be a way to drive them to the close button.

695. Address the objections your visitors are likely to have

Anticipate the questions and anxieties your visitors are likely to have and make sure you answer them on the page. This will help prevent people going elsewhere to find their answers and potentially finding a better offer.

696. Opt out

If someone is registering with you for a newsletter or ongoing communication, make it clear that they will be able to easily opt out at any time. Saying this up front is often the tipping point between someone saying "ok, sure" and "no way".

697. Remove the guesswork

Use Google Analytics to track your results immediately.

698. Basic metrics

You should ensure you are recording the fundamental performance metrics for each campaign. These are campaign specific, but can include: conversion rate (broad term), bounce/abandonment rate, form completion rate. Store these results so that you have a basis for showing how your refinement process (via A/B testing) is working, and to allow comparative reporting against previous campaigns that had the same goals.

699. Invest in eye tracking reports and heat mapping programmes

Eye tracking reports can give you valuable insight into where people are looking and help you increase the positioning of key elements. Heat mapping software can show heat map overlays showing where people are clicking most. Use this information to manipulate and test copy in the most popular areas to see if you can increase conversions. Other systems can produce a virtual heat map based on assumed attention areas based on graphical contrast and basic design patterns. All of these tools can add to your understanding of landing page behaviour.

700. Don't get complacent

Remember that there's always another percentage point of conversion waiting around the corner to be squeezed out of your customers. Keep testing and optimising your landing page until the campaign is finished.

701. Follow-up

After a conversion occurs, you must build on it. The more impressions you make on your customer, the more likely they are to remember your message. Something as simple as sending a thank you email will not only reinforce your message, but is used to get more information. When clients feel that you value their business, they will be more likely to come back or refer you to others.

Chapter 8

Video Marketing

In a Nutshell

Video adds a lot of muscle to your marketing and if you're not using videos to get your message across, make adding them to your marketing mix a priority. If you need convincing of the power of video, the following points should help:

- Only 20% of visitors actually read the text on a website whereas 80% of visitors will watch the exact same content on the same website in video form.

- Visitors who watch a video on a website stay two minutes longer than average and are 64% more likely to make a purchase.

- Google actually gives more weight to videos than standard web pages, especially YouTube videos.

The following tips will help to ensure your videos grab the interest and attention of your prospective customers or clients.

702. Make sure your video looks professional

Your video should project your company's image. Make sure it looks and sounds professional.

703. Use a brief introduction

Begin your video by telling people what the video is about and why they should be watching. For example, "Hi, it's [Your name] from [your company name]. In this short video I'm going to cover [the solution/insight or problem you'll solve]."

704. Tell people why they need to watch

Tell people very briefly why it's important they know what you're going to tell them.

705. Don't ramble on your video

Make your points concisely. Don't ramble – you'll annoy your viewers and lose their attention.

706. Cover one idea per video

Cover just one idea in your video. Solve one problem. Address one challenge you know your target audience has.

707. Talk to one person

Make it seem as if you're having a conversation with one person rather than a crowd of people. That will help your viewers to feel as if you're talking to them directly.

708. Keep the jargon to a minimum

Aim to make your video easy to understand. Your viewers probably won't know as much as you do.

709. Use a call to action

Ask people to share or comment on your video and take up your offer.

710. Use lighting effectively

No matter what option you choose for filming, the difference between high- and low-quality video content often comes down to lighting. It's critical to make sure that your video subjects are well lit by using basic lighting best practices. Achieving proper lighting is not difficult, but it's important to research various techniques (colour balancing, light placements, etc.) to ensure you get it right. You can also opt for natural light by shooting outside or in front of a window to keep the cost of production low.

711. Audio quality is critical

Whether you are shooting live footage or using simple voiceover narration, quality audio is critical. After all, the last thing you want is to distract your audience with echoes and static that can distort your message. In both cases, it's a good idea to invest in a quality microphone to record all audio. Clip-on microphones work best for talking head and interview content, while any simple microphone can drastically improve the quality of pre-recorded narration. In some cases, you may even want to invest in hiring professional voice talent to bring your audio to an even higher level.

712. Use background music

When used properly, background music can add a whole new dimension to your video content. This can include audio that is played as an intro or outro to your content, or music that plays continuously throughout. Just be careful to avoid issues with copyright laws when selecting music to include.

713. Keep your focus on your audience

Keep your target audience in mind throughout the planning and creation process. While working on videos with multiple people, it's easy for the tone and message of your video to change from what was originally intended. It's important to stay focused on the viewers you are trying to reach to ensure that your finished product gives you the best opportunity to reach your goals

714. Get your video professionally edited

Giving your videos a professional quality also requires proper editing and design. The editor should work closely with the script writer and videographer to ensure that the proper vision for the content is captured. The editor will be responsible for adding the appropriate visual elements (i.e. captions for talking heads, graphics for PowerPoint slides, etc.), background music, etc.

715. Use a script

For professional videos, it's helpful to have a script in place ahead of time. The writer should work with the subject matter expert and project manager to ensure the script is on-point and fully polished.

716. Add a video to your website homepage

People are naturally drawn to videos out of curiosity. Therefore, by placing a video on your homepage the visitor's attention will be instantly captured upon entering the site. This interest will then lead them to watch the video to see what it is all about.

717. Increase the time people spend watching

Once you have successfully obtained the viewer's attention, the next goal is to keep it. There are many interactive applications that you can add to your video that will engage the viewer and keep them interested longer. You can add a drop down box where they can gather additional information, a slide out box where they can link to other videos or a "sign up now" button that will take them to the next step. With each application you add to your video, you increase the visitor's time on your site. This is crucial, because those who spend more time on your site are usually the same ones who become customers.

718. Make sure your video is relevant to the content on the web page

Ensure the video you place on a web page or landing page is relevant to the text. There is nothing more annoying than for visitors to realise that the video has nothing to do with what they're looking for. Base your web page content on what relates to your target market specifically.

719. Consider your purpose and audience when deciding on the video's length

Although the total viewable length of a video isn't relevant to its entertainment value, it may prove to be a factor in attracting prospects to begin watching it. A short video of two to three minutes or less may entice a prospect to watch immediately.

Most people can spare a few minutes to watch a video on a topic that interests them. Longer videos, of more than five minutes, may wait in a prospect's inbox for a day or two until the person finds time to watch. A video lasting 15 minutes or longer may wait forever to be viewed, if the topic isn't particularly compelling and relevant to the prospect.

720. Break long, compelling messages into short videos

Break your long videos into smaller videos and label them 'Part 1', 'Part 2', 'Part 3' and so on. This strategy, which puts the power back into the viewer's hands, can effectively entice someone into taking action on your marketing appeal.

721. Your video doesn't have to 'go viral' to be successful

Instead of focusing on creating the next viral video, keep your focus on your overall goal of getting your message across to your target audience. Rather than aspire to attract millions of viewers, your goal should be to reach the people who comprise your target audience.

722. Offer more than one video

One video alone won't compel visitors to buy your products or hire your services. You need to create videos for several specific target audiences. A recent study indicates that companies successfully using video create 11 times more video than those that are unsuccessful with it.

723. Put videos where they can support your marketing messages

Place video in the logical place where it can best support your marketing message:

- If a video introduces your company, post the video on the homepage

- If a video explains a product in detail, add the video to the product page

- If a video contains a testimonial from a customer, place it next to the product it refers to or add it to your 'About Us' or 'Why You Should Choose Us' section

- If your video is related to an event, post the video in a blog article or news item that mentions it

724. Place your video where it will be easily spotted

Don't hide your video at the bottom of your website pages. Put it in a position where it will be the first thing your visitors see. Make sure visitors will see it without having to scroll down the page.

725. Use videos to support your content:

You can increase the effectiveness of links like 'learn more' by making a video of the target content. Write text, such as "Watch a video about product X," to see a likely increase in clicks on these items. The link opens a separate page where viewers can see the video and you can place calls to action and other content directly on the page.

726. Do place videos on your product pages

Video is probably the best way to explain and demonstrate products.

727. Use videos on your testimonials page

If you use customer testimonials to market products (and you should), ask a few customers to appear in a video testimonial. Filmed testimonials have much more credibility than simple text-based testimonials because people know they're much harder to fake.

728. Use video case studies

Attract new prospects by demonstrating how existing customers use your product.

729. Interview experts for your blog

Support your blog posts with videos showing expert interviews, short reports from your company events or trade shows, and in-depth educational content.

730. Place conversion elements close to your video

Make it easy for your website visitors to take the next action by placing conversion elements close to the video. Examples of frequently used conversion elements are:

- Contact information

- Conversion forms

- In-player lead capture

- Live chat (to allow viewers to ask you any questions they may have after watching the video)

731. Create a dedicated video section if you have lots of video content

Bundle all video content so that people can easily find it. If you have a lot of videos and you know that your users value your video content highly, having a dedicated video section can make sense.

732. Use videos on your landing pages

Landing pages are dedicated web pages that are designed to capture leads. Most ads online link not to a company's homepage, but to a landing page that provides focused information about the subject of the ad. Most landing pages also contain online forms where prospects can immediately sign up for a newsletter, download collateral, and white papers, or request more information. Such pages can benefit tremendously from integrated videos.

Useful content, well-written headlines and an attractive design are essential, but there's no quicker and more effective way to attract attention than with a well-placed video. Some studies suggest that video landing pages can achieve a 60 to 100% higher conversion rate than traditional text-only pages.

733. Make sure your landing page video relates to whatever you're promoting

Your landing page videos must be directly connected to the topic of your landing page. If you place only a generic company video on a landing page that's pitching one of your products, the video won't be effective. If you're pitching product 'X', feature that product (and not much else) in the video. People expect fast, focused information from landing pages, and that's what entices them to convert. Make your landing page videos short, to the point, and attractive.

734. Turn off YouTube's related videos

If you use YouTube's hosting service for your website videos, it will offer a selection of related videos at the end of your video. To turn off the list of related videos that show up at the end of your YouTube-hosted video, try this trick: find the video URL in the embed code of your video from the YouTube site then add the characters ?rel=0 immediately afterward. When you use this changed embed code, the related videos disappear.

735. Use an attractive thumbnail image

A useful thumbnail picture conveys what the video is about. The thumbnail should look immediately attractive and appealing. Show people and faces rather than static objects. You can even edit the thumbnail picture to add text to make your pitch about why people should watch this video.

736. Add the 'Play' button on top of your thumbnail picture

People have learned to look for the 'Play' button to identify videos. You're likely to reduce your video play rates if you don't have one.

737. Use only one video per web page

If you have 10 videos, make 10 individual web pages.

Search engines ignore multiple videos per page, and having multiple videos dilutes the effectiveness of your SEO efforts. If you do want to offer visitors several videos on a page to engage them more however, create pages with those individual videos that are visible only to search engines.

738. Supply a descriptive title for your web pages and use a keyword-rich URL

Rather than post the video on the page, add text that accurately describes the content of the video.

739. Optimise your videos

One of the best ways to naturally aid your video's search rankings is to make sure your video's metadata (title, tags, description, annotations and closed captions) are as optimised as possible.

740. Get backlinks to your YouTube channel

Every time you comment on another video you get a backlink to your channel. To find videos to comment on, search YouTube for popular videos (videos with lots of views) closely related to your uploaded videos. Leave a non spammy comment on up to 10 related videos a day. If you leave comments on more than 10 a day, Google's algorithms may put you down as a spammer.

741. Keep your comments on other people's videos simple

Don't promote your channel or your videos in the comments, simply say what you thought of the video, or reply to someone else's comment. When you leave the comment your name appears blue and becomes a hyperlink (backlink) to your channel, so make sure you are logged into your main YouTube account. Once done, ping the URLs of all the videos you left comments on so Google indexes your backlinks.

742. Boost the chances of your video appearing next to high traffic videos

Find a similar video to yours with a lot of views then use keywords from that video's title as some of the tags for your video. Make sure the keywords you choose are closely related to your own video. This will tell YouTube that your video is closely related to the video with lots of views. Therefore your video is more likely to appear on the related videos list, alongside the video with lots of views. Videos with a high view count will get a vast number of daily views and if your video appears in the related videos list next to those videos, your video will get a significant portion of those views every day.

743. Use a video to add interest to your FAQ page

The Frequently Asked Questions (FAQ) is an important part of any website but it can often be the most boring part too. Make your FAQ page more interesting with videos. A few short videos that answer the most important questions can help significantly.

744. Transform your learning section

If you have an educational section on your website, offer video as well as text resources. Video is one of the most effective ways to provide educational content that people appreciate and share with others.

745. Use a video on your About Us page

Most visitors will look at the About Us page of a website before making the decision to buy a product or use a service. You can make your About Us section more memorable with a short, interesting video.

746. Make videos highly visible

Place videos directly on the web pages rather than hiding them behind hard to find links. Make it easy for people to see them.

747. Use a thumbnail image rather than pop-up video players

Steer clear of pop-up video players. Studies have shown that such players decrease viewership. Use a thumbnail image that plays the video when selected.

748. Get your thumbnails right

Getting your thumbnails right is vital to attract as many new viewers as possible. Thumbnails are the number one thing that draws people to click on a video, way more than the title and description. Very recently YouTube has made it so that all monetised accounts can upload a custom thumbnail for their videos. To do this click "Edit" next to your video on the "Video Manager" page, then click "Custom Thumbnail", and it will let you select any image from your computer to use as a thumbnail.

749. Don't forget other video sites

YouTube is the biggest online video site but there are hundreds of smaller, yet well-established video hosts that are worth using too. By distributing your videos across different video sites, not only will you get more views but you will also get lots of backlinks. You can use these backlinks to push your YouTube video up the YouTube and, even better, Google search rankings. To do this copy and paste the URL of one of your YouTube videos into the descriptions of your videos on all the other video sharing sites. The goal is to get all of the videos you uploaded to other video sites backlinking to your YouTube videos. Because YouTube is where the majority of the traffic is, it is important to focus your backlinking efforts on your YouTube videos.

The other video hosting sites include: Dailymotion, Metacafe, Myspace, Vimeo, videobash and flickr.

You can upload your videos to all of these sites manually or outsource the task. There are also online software solutions that will automatically upload all your videos to a selection of video sharing sites for a monthly fee.

750. Organise the videos on your YouTube channel into playlists

This helps people find what they want quickly without having to scroll through a wall of videos. Playlists also help with your channel's SEO since Google uses the name of your playlists as a ranking signal for certain keywords. For example, if someone types keywords in Google that you have used in your playlist, your playlist might appear somewhere in the search results, which means more traffic to your channel. The more popular your channel becomes, the more it will happen.

When creating playlists for your videos think of the playlists like separate television shows, and the videos like episodes in the series. This is how YouTube wants you to build your channel, because YouTube's goal is to emulate how television works but in a more user friendly and instant format.

751. Associate your website with your YouTube channel

You can associate your channel's website with your channel itself. This will tell YouTube where viewers can find the official online website for your channel. YouTube and Google use the content on your website as a ranking signal for your channel and all the videos on it. This can help your video to get a higher ranking, providing that your channel's associated website has quality, relevant content and is updated often.

To associate your website with your channel, click "Channel Settings' in your YouTube dashboard then "Advanced", and then type your website's URL, including the leading http:// into the box under "Associated Website" and click "Add". You will then be required to verify that you own the website. Follow the simple instructions provided to verify domain ownership.

752. Keep your video title simple

The title of your video must be short and snappy but contain all the relevant words to tell your audience what the video is about. Your title should not be over complicated.

753. Add eye catching words in brackets before or after your video title

Help your video title to stand out by adding eye catching and intriguing words in brackets, before or after your title.

754. Make your video tags concise and relevant

Use between six to eight relevant keywords to create your video tags. Stuffing your tags with any old keywords will actually have a negative effect on your video's search rankings. Each tag should be as relevant to your video's content as possible; avoid unnecessary additive words.

755. Choose words that people are likely to use to search

When trying to think up your video's tags, think to yourself "What would I type in the search box if I wanted to find my video?"

756. Use key contact information in your video description

The start of your description should contain key contact information to boost your social followings, such as your Twitter, Facebook, Google Plus and tumblr pages.

For example:

- like me on Facebook: https://facebook.com/myPage,

- follow me on Twitter: http://twitter.com/myTwitterUsername,

- check out my blog: http://myBlog.tumblr.com.

757. Save yourself time

Once you've written the social networking part of your description, copy and paste it into a text file for future reference, then any time you post a new video all you have to do is open up the file and paste it into your description.

758. Make sure you mention your website in your description

Tell people where they can find you outside of YouTube. This should always be at or near the start of your description and any other information should follow it.

759. Use a detailed video description

For best SEO results, your video's description should contain keywords related to your business, contact details and a link to your website.

760. Fill your description with your audio transcript

One way to fill your description is to transcribe the audio from your video into a script and paste it into your description. Google's duplicate content rules also apply to YouTube videos, so ensure all the content in your description (and video) is over 90% unique. If transcribing is something that fills you with dread, outsource the task.

761. Make sure all your thumbnails look different

Your video thumbnails need to stand out from the crowd. Make them bright, bold and unique.

762. Timestamp your videos

If your videos have lots of scenes, timestamp them. It enables your viewers to find the part of the video they came to see much quicker and easier.

763. Encourage comments

Ask your audience a thought-provoking or controversial question at the end of every video to encourage comments. It will increase your video's YouTube and Google presence and engage your audience with your channel. It will also give you lots of ideas for future videos. Your questions should be as easy for your audience to answer as possible.

764. Create a YouTube channel for each niche you serve

Most YouTube channels focus on a specific niche or genre of video. If you have more than one niche to explore you should create a separate, uniquely branded channel for each niche. You can always cross-promote all your channels in your videos.

765. Create a screen capture tutorial

Create a simple PowerPoint presentation and then record what's on your computer screen, with software such as Camtasia or Screenflow, as you talk over the slide presentation. This type of video suits:

- Product demos

- Sales videos

- Technical training.

766. Create customer testimonials

This is one of the most powerful forms of video marketing. Ask your best customers or clients to provide a very brief 30-second talk about why they love your products or services.

767. Make your customer testimonial videos easy to edit

Ask your customers to begin their video testimonials with the phrase "The reason I really like/love [your product/service name]..." This will make it easier to edit their response in context.

768. Use Skype if you sell products/services virtually

If you sell products or services virtually, record people on Skype talking about your company, or have them leave a voice mail message, and put that into a video with a simple slideshow.

769. Do a video question and answer session

Just ask people what their biggest questions/ frustrations are... and then answer them.

770. Identify the best keywords for your video

Use the Google Keyword Planner tool. Click on "Search for new keyword and ad group ideas". Enter a couple of keywords related to your video topics. Hit "Get Ideas". Click on the "Keyword Ideas" tab. Hit "search" again. Start browsing the "Keyword Ideas" to find keyword phrases that have at least 1500 local searches a month. Find a keyword that matches your video, and fit it into your video title somehow.

771. Don't put the keyword phrase at the end of the video title

Place your keyword phrase at the beginning of your video title.

772. Rename your video file according to your keyword

The name of your video file directly relates to its ranking and relevancy in YouTube so name it the keyword you want to rank for. You have to change the video's name on your computer, before you upload it to YouTube. Just click on the folder until the folder name is highlighted, and type in the keyword.

773. Make sure your YouTube channel is niche-focused

Create a YouTube channel using one of the keywords for your market.

774. Write a great description for your video

The description of your YouTube video influences how your video ranks in the search engines. Your description needs to have four parts and it must be in this order:

1) A hyperlink to your website. (This must be first, and it must include the http://…

2) Repeat the offer you made in the video.

3) Describe your video. You are given 1,000 characters and use as much of that as you can. Make sure you include your keyword.

4) Provide your contact details. Repeat the offer and your hyperlink.

775. Use your competitors' video tags

One of the key factors in ranking your video is the tags, and the relationship those tags have to the other top related videos in your subject.

Find out what video has the top ranking for that keyword (search in YouTube under that phrase and find out who comes out at the top).

Click on the top YouTube video for the phrase you want to rank for. As the video is playing, right-click on your mouse and choose "View Page Source". Lots of code will appear. Press 'Control' and 'F' on your keyboard and put in "keywords". This will highlight the area of the code related to keywords.

Let's say that you're looking at professional service providers in London. An area that says something like: "< meta name =" keywords" content =" professional service providers London" >. Grab everything in the "professional service providers London" space after the "content =".

776. Promote your video everywhere

Once you upload your video on YouTube, you will get a unique URL. With that web address, you can now promote that video on social networks like Facebook, LinkedIn, Twitter, Pinterest, tumblr, your email newsletter, etc. Ask people to "like" it or "share" it when they watch the video. (Lots of social activity around your video, especially when it's first uploaded, is a big sign to Google that this video is "important" and should be given a prominent place in the search engines.)

777. Send out a press release to promote your video

Write a headline that is focused on the problem you're solving. Write it in the third person. Make sure you include links back to the video, along with the keywords you're using.

778. Create annotations

Annotations are a way to add linkable text overlays on to your video. You can use them to:

- Encourage people to subscribe to your YouTube channel

- Provide links to your other videos

- Link over to other YouTube users' videos who offer further resources

To create them, click on the annotations button below your video then let the video play to the point where you want the annotation. Add the annotation.

779. Create keyword friendly playlists

Create a playlist around a specific keyword that includes your videos and a mix of other people's videos. Don't include your competitor's videos.

780. Respond to comments within 24 hours

One of the biggest factors in determining the "authority" of your YouTube channel is your engagement with people who leave comments, especially within a day or so of the comment being left. Check-in every couple of days to respond to comments. (You should get an email each time a comment is left.)

Don't bother responding to negative comments – it's a waste of your time.

781. Build your subscriber list quickly

Send messages to your target audience inviting them to check out your new video and/ or subscribe to your channel.

Just search for videos related to your subject. Find people who've left a comment in the past two months. Click on their name to bring up their profile page.

Click on the "send message" button. Create a friendly message that says something like, "I see that you're interested in/a fan of [the subject of the video]. I just made a video of [the subject of your video]. I thought you'd like to see it. Thank you!"

782. Use external annotations

Go to your YouTube channel settings. Click on 'monetization'. (Follow the steps laid out by YouTube.) Add your website. Click on associated website under Channel Settings.

Go back to the video you want to add the annotation to. Click "annotations." When you add the annotation in your video check the "link" box. Add your website in the field provided. Save changes. This is a great way to drive more traffic back to your website.

783. Create and submit a video sitemap

Since video is indexed differently than text-based content in Google, you can increase the online visibility of your videos by putting together a video sitemap in addition to a standard sitemap.

This will essentially help Google identify which content items on your site are videos, while providing the search engine with more information on what your content is about so it can be indexed properly.

Keep in mind, however, that developing a video sitemap requires some fields that are a bit more technical in nature than those of a standard sitemap, so content creators should work with their webmaster or web development teams.

784. Use the word 'video' in your email subject line

Some studies have shown that simply including the word "video" in an email's subject line can increase click-through rates by as much as 13%.

785. Promote your webinars using videos

Video is a great tool for promoting product updates and general company details via email, but can also be a very effective form of webinar marketing. For example, many companies have found success creating short "trailers" for upcoming events. These work in a similar way to film promotions in that they quickly inform viewers of the content to be covered (usually less than two minutes), all the while driving registrations ahead of time.

786. Make sure the link to your webinar trailer video stands alone

Don't embed it within the text of your email. This will make it easier for recipients to see what your email is about and know exactly what to do from there.

787. If your trailer is short (and it should be), say so in the hyperlink

Something like "View this 45-second trailer to learn more" might encourage a higher click-through rate, as it lets people know that the video won't take up much of their time.

788. Share your video on Twitter

Sharing video content via social channels is another great way to extend the reach of your content and encourage audience engagement. Due to the high volume of information shared on Twitter, don't be afraid to share the same content multiple times.

If you only post your video once, you risk it being ignored or lost amidst all the chatter. Posting multiple times over the span of a week or month not only increases your video's visibility, but also allows you to experiment with new messaging around the same content to learn what works best.

789. Don't flood your Facebook page with too much video content

Flooding your Facebook page with too much content can turn off your audience, causing them to tune you out, or worse yet, stop following you.

790. Use video on LinkedIn

LinkedIn users are often more receptive to business-related content and messaging, and video can give you a major advantage. Start your own LinkedIn group to post video content with current and prospective customers. Join other industry-related groups to share thought leadership videos with new prospects and influencers.

791. Make your videos mobile friendly

Keep videos short. This is especially important for mobile viewers who lack a high-speed connection and tend to have an even shorter attention span than those using PCs. As with other mediums, paid video ads tend to be no longer than 30 seconds, while other content intended for mobile viewing should stay right around the "two minutes or less" mark.

792. Use larger graphics and images for mobile friendly videos

The small screen size of mobile phones is not ideal for lots of small text and numbers. Keep this mind when designing your content by using visuals that are easy to consume and understand, no matter what device the viewer is using.

793. Use Quick Response (QR) codes

One of the most popular ways for companies to get their videos out in front of a mobile audience these days is through the use of QR codes. Customers can scan the codes with their mobile devices to view additional content, webpages, demos or videos.

794. Measure the impact of your videos

There are certain key metrics to monitor in terms of your videos. The most basic metric to monitor is views.

A view is achieved anytime someone clicks to play your video.

Some analytics tools also allow you to filter out unique views (the number of singular people who have watched the video at least once), which can also have value.

Total views make up the easiest way to determine the popularity of your videos, the effectiveness of your messaging and your ability to entice people to click on your content.

However, it's important to keep certain variables in mind that can skew these numbers, such as the amount of promotion a video receives and whether the content is geared toward a broad or specific audience.

795. Monitor click-throughs

One of the goals of video marketing is to draw viewers to your company's call to action. Most often, this level of engagement is based on encouraging viewers to click through from your video to additional pages on your company site, or to sign up for a demo or upcoming event.

In this case, URL tracking codes offer a simple way to track how successful your videos are at moving viewers further down the lead funnel. A tracking code can easily be described as a simple identifier added to the end of a typical URL. For email marketing campaigns, these tracking codes can be generated automatically via integration with marketing automation systems. In other cases, they can simply be added manually to the end of a clean URL and tracked in Google Analytics.

796. Improve online videos with keywords

The number of times that you use a keyword in your online video makes a difference to its success. Your keyword should be included in your title as well as your description. Your keywords should take up about 3% of the text. At the same time, you need to ensure that you don't overload your content with the keyword.

797. Make sure recipients can find the video in your email

Make video the main focus of an email. It can't get lost in the text of a newsletter, for example. Since video can be more costly to create than text and static graphic emails, you need to make the focus the video to drive engagement.

798. Be careful with the quality of videos you use in emails

Your videos shouldn't look like they've been made in a hurry or too cheaply. It might be great for your budget, but if you're not making quality content, you risk hurting your brand.

799. Remember to use a clear call to action in videos in emails

Failing to include a specific action to take within the video could lose you potential leads. You can't just send people to a web page. You do need to create an actionable experience.

800. Use a reliable hosting service

When you are marketing your video, the last thing you want is an unreliable hosting service that ruins your efforts. It's important to use a provider that will offer you consistent quality and give you the assurance that your video won't be spontaneously taken down at any point.

Websites such as YouTube and Vimeo are traditionally pretty reasonable at providing such a service; if you want 100% peace of mind, then investing some money into a host might be a good idea.

801. Remember to tell viewers your name

Don't leave viewers guessing as to whose video they've just watched. Let them know your brand name. Viewers need to see your brand; they need to know who's behind the video. If you produce a great video and give yourself no credit, viewers might mistake your competitor as the creator of your service or product.

Chapter 9

Email Marketing

In A Nutshell

A survey of marketing professionals in both B2C and B2B companies around the world[4] found that they consider email marketing more effective than marketing techniques like paid search or online ads, SEO, content marketing, direct mail or print ads, offline events like trade shows, social media marketing, online events like webinars, or mobile marketing.

Email is still one of the cheapest and yet most effective marketing tools that you can use to communicate directly with your prospective, existing and past clients. You can respond immediately to their request for information, you can contact old clients, communicate with your existing clients, distribute press releases, send invitations to prospects to visit your website, and alert prospects and clients alike about new services, sales, discounts, seminars, and special events, etc. However, the low cost, high returns and convenience of email marketing means that many other companies are using it for the same reason. The result: the inboxes of your prospects and clients get clogged up and all but a few messages are deleted without being read.

Your challenge therefore is to create email messages that stand out amid the clutter of those crowded email boxes and that get opened, read and acted upon.

---

[4] 'Lead Generation Strategy Outlook Report', Ascend2, April 18, 2013.

If people don't even open your emails, you'll never accomplish your goal.

You know you'll never get 100% of recipients to open your emails. However, you can monitor from one email campaign to the next whether there's a difference in open rates. If it rises, you know you've got things right. If it falls, you know there's a problem.

802. Customise your 'from' field for maximum recognition

Take advantage of the customisable 'from' field in most email delivery systems and make it work for you.

803. Personalise your emails

Organisations that use email personalisation techniques achieve 57% higher average order values than those who send generic emails to everyone on their mailing list.

804. Personalise the email subject line

Writing personalised subject lines (which use the name of the recipient) almost doubles the likelihood of your email being opened.

805. Experiment with your subject line

Try different subject lines and see what works best. Some experts recommend using numbers in the subject line to increase readership and response rates.

806. Keep your subject line short and snappy

Two reasons here: (1) many email clients limit the subject line to about 30 characters anyway, and (2) it's just good marketing sense to make your point in as few words as possible.

807. Know your readers and tune your subject line to them

Industry standards convey that most men prefer subject lines that communicate news or compelling information, while most women prefer discount offers. Leverage current market research to fine-tune your subject line.

808. Send your email to yourself

Send an email to yourself and pretend you are one of your readers. How does it look in your inbox? Would you open it?

809. Make it easy to 'white list' your emails

Consider including a common word, perhaps your newsletter name, in square brackets [Splash] at the beginning of your subject line so readers can use a filter based on that word, or clear your emails with IT or their ISP, to avoid sending your emails into the spam bucket.

810. Be aware of timing

If you publish your email in the early hours of the morning, it will appear in your recipients' inboxes first thing in the morning along with possibly hundreds of other emails. If you publish too late in the day, you run the risk that your recipient will delete it in the rush to leave the office. Ask your readers what time is best for them.

811. Make your subject lines provocative, original or intriguing

Imagine your prospect or client with an email inbox crammed full of headlines that look the same. Yours must stand out. Hook your reader in with something that jumps out and virtually pulls them into your email.

812. Keep your eye on the goal

The ultimate aim of your autoresponder sequence is to build trust with your prospects and continue to build a relationship with your clients and so help you to increase your sales.

813. Prospect vs client email content

You want your prospect to get to know, like and trust you so that they will feel comfortable doing business with you – so give them useful information. To encourage your clients to continue doing business with you (think of all those up-sell, down-sell and cross-sell opportunities) after they've bought from you, provide them with reassurance that they've made a great decision, and then give them step-by-step information about how to get the best from the service they've invested in.

814. Target your market

Know the fears, needs, desires or wants that your clients/prospects have and how your service meets/solves/resolves them. Write down 10 of their biggest problems, fears, needs or wants. They will become the themes of your automated email messages. Use one theme per message. At least one of those top 10 will hit the 'trigger buttons' of your prospect.

815. Don't use a sledgehammer to put a nail in

Think of offering information rather than a blatant sales pitch. Provide useful information and be subtle with your 'sales' message. Think of getting clicks to your landing page rather than trying to sell in the email.

816. Hook them in and don't let them go

Jay White, autoresponder expert, says your opening statements should be "an eyeball pulling opener". If you're stuck for ideas, use the 5 'W's so beloved of journalists – who, what, why, when and where– let your reader know who you are, why you're writing to them, what you're writing about, where you're from and why they should carry on reading.

817. Focus on your reader not yourself

Your email message must be about your client not you.

818. Go easy on the name thing

Use your client or prospect's name once or twice at the most in the email. More than that is going to seem unnatural and slightly creepy.

819. Always make regular contact with prospects

Send your first welcome and congratulations type message immediately after your prospect has opted-in. It should be a strong message. Keep in regular contact or follow up with regular autoresponders to make sure that your company is always at the top of your prospects' minds.

820. No wide loads

To make your emails easy to read, keep the lines to about 55 characters in length. Keep your subject lines under 20 characters.

821. Use an audio link in your emails

Place the audio link at the top of your message so people who prefer to listen rather than read can still access your information. The link will take them to a page where they can play/stream your email.

822. Make it personal

Think of your autoresponder message as a one-to-one communication. Use conversational language – be liberal with contractions (like 'you're', 'don't' and 'we'll'). Don't be afraid to start a sentence with 'and' or 'but'.

823. Think Goldilocks

Your message shouldn't be too long or too short – like Goldilocks' porridge, it should be 'just right'. Tell a story, press your prospects' trigger buttons (their overwhelming need/want/desire), highlight the benefits of your service, and close.

824. Take action!

Do have a call to action in all of your emails. What do you want your readers to do after reading your message? Do you want them to follow the link to your website? To call your office? Make it clear – tell your readers exactly what steps you want them to take. Let them know in a compelling, benefits-oriented way why it's in their best interest to take action immediately.

825. And rest...

A strong and persuasive sequence of email messages can help you boost sales and save you time, energy, and money! Let those auto responders get to work for you!

826. Test what works for your audience

What works for one company, might not work for your company. What works today might not work next week. That's why it's best to test everything to see what does and does not work in emails for your target audience.

827. Determine the best times to send out emails

Some email experts will tell you that emails sent before and after working hours get the best open rates. Others will tell you that Mondays, Wednesday and Fridays are best while a few will heartily recommend weekend email blasts. The best way of finding out what works for your target audience is to test it. Do an A/B split on your email blast (mailing) and send half in the morning, half in the afternoon and see if one responds better than the other. Do this several times to see if you can determine a pattern. Try different weekdays then weekends. Measure your results. Keep testing.

828. Test HTML and text versions of the same email

Text may be ugly, but it can still be very effective.

829. If the first email does not succeed, send it again

Very often response is better on the resend (and resend of the resend) than on the original deployment. If you don't get a positive response and instead find that you get an unusual rise in unsubscribes as a result of sending the same email out then don't risk repeating the exercise. Your email recipients have told you what they think of your efforts and you'd be silly to ignore the message they've giving you.

830. Limit the number of images you send in an email

Make sure your HTML does not have too many images because this can cause spam filters to go into overdrive.

831. Try the 'f' word in your emails

The word 'free' is supposed to send spam filters into overdrive but test the 'f' word yourself and see what happens.

832. Understand the 'fields'

'Fields' are what prospects see when an email arrives in their inbox. They give a hint of what's inside. Fields of most concern to email marketers are the 'FROM' field, the 'TO' field, and the 'SUBJECT' field.

833. Target. Target. Target.

The more you customise your email to specific target groups, the more successful your efforts will be.

834. Focus on building the relationship

Email marketing is not a hit and run medium. It works best when you use it to build sustainable relationships with prospects and customers. So, each time you write an email marketing message, remember that you're building a relationship as well as trying to generate a lead, hit, or sale. Building a solid relationship with your email marketing list will lead to higher response rates in future campaigns.

835. Don't use people's first names in the subject line every time

Using people's first names in the subject lines may boost your sales a couple of times but it's a mistake to use their names every time you email them. After all, colleagues and friends don't use each other's first names in subject lines every time they make contact, do they?

836. Offer information for free

Teaching in your emails can be an invaluable way of building a relationship with a prospect. When you're offering information for free, don't make it too promotional – just focus on building the relationship.

837. Plan for rapid fulfilment

Make sure you have all the internal resources in place to handle fulfilment of premiums, leads and other responses to your email marketing campaign. Slow fulfilment will backfire horribly on you.

838. It's a game of two halves

An email marketing campaign has two parts, not one: the email your customer receives, plus the hyperlink embedded in the email that he or she clicks on to respond to your offer. This link takes the customer to a web page with a reply form (the landing page). The landing page requires as much attention to writing and design as the email itself.

839. Avoid using ALL CAPS

Avoid the temptation to add emphasis to your words by using all caps. It is fine for one or two areas but don't overdo it. It looks too blatant. What's more, online all caps are considered the equivalent of shouting. You wouldn't shout at a client if they were standing in front of you, would you?

840. Go easy on the exclamation marks

Never overuse exclamations in any form of marketing communication but especially in email marketing. That's because the "!" symbol is used as a spam filter in many email software programmes and because it adds little to the power of your email message. It may even diminish its impact.

841. No long paragraphs

Long paragraphs are intimidating. A rule of thumb for sales letters and other marketing materials is that no paragraph should be longer than seven lines. In email marketing, keep paragraphs in your email to six lines or less. This will make the text look concise and more inviting to read.

842. Use a standard letter format

Start with a salutation and end with a signature. Remember, email is personal communication – even more personal these days than mail delivered by post. If you don't use a standard letter format, your email message will look impersonal and promotional.

843. When to use non-letter formats

In some forms of email marketing– such as catalogue updates, special announcements and email newsletters (ezines) – a standard letter format is not necessary.

844. Don't send advertising

Don't design your email message to look like a print advertisement or banner ad. Just because these are effective in other media doesn't mean they will perform well in an email. Usually, they won't, and will only prove to irritate your target market. Write for the medium.

845. Watch the margins

If your email programme has this option, set the margins for outgoing email to 20 and 80.This will make the text easier to read. If you don't have this option, consider manually returning (pressing the 'Enter' button) each line at about 55 characters (an average of 12 words.) This will present your text attractively without displaying any strange or ugly line breaks.

846. Choose the most readable fonts

The best fonts for email communications are Arial 10pt and Verdana 10pt. Never go smaller than 10pt under any circumstance. If you decide to send your email message in 12pt, use Arial.

To apply for a free implementation session **worth £495** where we show you how everything in this book can be done for you, go to **completedigitalmarketingsystem.com/121**

237

847. Steer clear of jokes or puns

Be conversational and friendly but don't joke. It's all too easy for jokes and puns to be misinterpreted.

848. Don't send file attachments

File attachments of any kind should be avoided in email marketing. This is because few recipients will open an email file attachment from an unfamiliar source. If you have information to share that requires a file attachment, turn it into a web page instead. Then add a hyperlink to it from within your email marketing message.

849. Use a conversational voice

The best writing style for this medium is conversational and to the point. Just be sure you understand your target market enough to apply the appropriate tonality.

850. Address an audience of one rather than many

To make your email personal, write each one as if you're addressing one person rather than many.

851. Make it personal

If possible, use a personal name in the FROM line of your message. This reinforces the one-to-one, friendly tone your message must have to be successful.

852. Make someone the face of your business

Don't use your company name to sign off emails. Instead, take an individual in your company and make them the face of the business, so that people get used to receiving emails from a human being.

853. The subject line is critical to your email's success

Your customers and prospects will base much of their decision on whether or not to open your email based on what is written in the

SUBJECT line. Like the headline of a print ad, the SUBJECT line copy is vital to the success of your email marketing efforts. Spend time crafting your subject line.

854. You don't have much room for the subject

Realistically, you have only about 60 characters in the subject field. That's usually less than nine words. The words you choose must be sufficiently attention-grabbing and intriguing to stand out on a page of other subject lines. That's a Herculean task so it's imperative you put some effort into choosing the right words.

855. Ask a question

Asking a question in your subject line can be a good way of ensuring it gets clicked on. Just be sure your question is honest and straightforward – not cryptic, hyped, or suspicious.

856. Avoid cryptic or clever phrases in your subject line

These rarely work with email. What arouses curiosity or intrigue on a printed envelope may be greeted with suspicion when used in the SUBJECT field of an email.

857. Avoid hype and empty promises

Hype rarely works anyway. Such marketing messages are usually greeted with scepticism and deleted.

858. Teasers work well

An attention-grabbing teaser works very well in email – perhaps more so than in conventional direct mail.

859. Start with the benefit

Highlighting the key benefit of your offer can be effective in the SUBJECT field. This is provided you can do so effectively in just seven to nine words. Just be sure to avoid a promotional or hyped tone. State your benefit simply.

To apply for a free implementation session **worth £495** where we show you how everything in this book can be done for you, go to completedigitalmarketingsystem.com/121

239

860. Use a deadline

If there is a time limit to your offer, including this in the SUBJECT field can be motivating. For example: "Subject: Renewal notice. Deadline noon tomorrow."

861. Remind them they asked for it

It can be frustrating for marketers when customers ask to receive information or notifications – and then don't read the subsequent email. In these cases, remind your recipients in the SUBJECT field that this is requested information. People forget.

862. Always use a salutation

Although it's an informal medium, some marketers make the mistake of being too casual. Like any good sales letter, always greet your customer or prospect with a friendly salutation.

863. If you can, personalise

If available and practical, always begin your email message with the proper name of the recipient. Use both the first name and last name if possible. Test what works best for your audience.

864. Use traditional headlines with care

Headlines in sales letters can work well in conventional direct mail packages. But their influence is diminished in email marketing. This doesn't mean you shouldn't use headlines. In some email campaigns, you should. You just need to realise that headlines are not as powerful in this medium.

865. Work hard on the opening sentence

The opening sentence of your email message will either draw readers in or turn them off to the extent they delete the entire message. You need to craft it with great care.

866. The opening sentence should stand alone

Starting an email marketing message with a standalone sentence – rather than a multi-sentence paragraph –works well. Consider asking a question, quoting an unusual and interesting statistic, or highlighting your offer. These types of opening sentences make it easier for your audience to get into the copy. It makes the opening look a less intimidating read than beginning with a full paragraph.

867. Focus on the first few lines

Many people set their email programmes to display the first few lines of their email message. This is especially the case for people viewing business emails – they do it so they can see at a glance whether or not the message is worth further reading. That's why you should really focus on making the first few lines of your email message as engaging and relevant as possible. What do you want your prospect to see that will persuade him or her to read further?

868. Apply the 5-30 rule to your email messages

The 5-30 rule is you tell the five-second version of your marketing message then you tell the 30-second version. The mini five-second version of your story should be at the top of your email. It needs to be short and concise, containing a couple of the key benefits along with the offer and response instructions. This will appeal to those with short attention spans and others who don't like to scroll.

869. Get to the point quickly

Unlike conventional direct mail in which you can take a little time to get to the point, in email marketing, you must get to the main point fast.

870. Mention the offer in the first few sentences

You need to state the offer right on top, preferably within the first few sentences of your email message. If you force recipients to scroll down to get to the gist of your message, you risk losing them. Email marketing messages with the offer stated on top pull better than those with the offer highlighted only at the end.

871. Highlight the main benefits at the top of the email message

Highlight the main benefits at the top of your email message. If there is more than one key benefit, use a bullet list, but keep that list to three points maximum. Don't be afraid to be quick and brief with the benefits at the top of your email message. You can always go into more detail further down.

872. Tell people what to do in the first few sentences

Never state the offer without associating it with the response instructions. In email marketing, the most popular method of response is clicking a hyperlink (embedded in the email message) to a web page. Freephone numbers are also an option, but don't get the same response as hyperlinks since internet users prefer to click rather than pick up the phone.

873. Highlight the offer and the response instructions in the middle of the message

You must sell the offer and provide clear response instructions in the body of your email message – even if you already did this in the opening few sentences. Since your message body contains expanded information, this will appeal to those who make a decision only after learning more details. You want to avoid a situation where they have to scroll up and down the page to find out how to respond.

874. Don't be afraid to go long

For some offers at least, longer copy that tells a more complete story does better than short copy. This is especially true when a transaction is involved, such as a subscription or sign-up.

875. Break the key messages into sections

Your message should be comprised of short paragraphs, subheads, and bullets. This improves readability and makes the text, especially longer text, appear less intimidating.

876. Write for people who like to scan

People tend to scan email before reading it word-for-word, even more so than in print communication. So, make sure a reader can gain a clear understanding of your message from the fields, opening sentence, subheads and bullets.

877. Check the links

If you put a hyperlink in your email, check it before you send it then check it again. Links that don't work reflect poorly on your organisation and irritate readers.

878. Always include a signature

Email is a personal, one-to-one communication, which means that the email is not only directed to someone, but from someone as well: always include a signature.

879. When you can't personalise a signature, use 'team' instead

Sometimes it is inappropriate or impractical to include a personalised signature complete with a proper name. In this case, consider using the word "team" in its place.

880. Advertise below the signature

Although your email as a whole should not look like advertising, you can get away with a promotional blurb incorporated into the signature. Below the name in the signature you can include your website address, a recent special offer (for example: "Click here for a 10% discount..."), links to new product information, a current promotion, and, of course, your company slogan or tagline.

881. Always hyperlink the call to action

Most prospects will click on a hyperlink in your email message to respond to your offer. If you don't have a hyperlink, response will suffer dramatically

882. Add a Freephone number

While most prospects will respond to your offer online by clicking a link, some will prefer to call and speak with someone live. Encourage those who prefer to call to take action by offering them a Freephone number.

883. Place a hyperlink on the top, in the middle and at the bottom

Most click-through responses will come from the hyperlink at the top, bottom, and middle of your email message – in that order. Make sure you include hyperlinks in these positions.

884. Keep it simple

State the response instructions simply in clear, everyday language. Ask people within your organisation to check the messages you send out to ensure each one is clear and understandable.

885. Link to more information

Create a link to more in-depth information existing on a web page. Just be sure to include a link back to your offer on that web page. You don't want to lose your readers to other distractions which could see them leave your website for further browsing.

886. Don't use email forms

Avoid designing a form within your email for users to respond to. Very few will fill it out. Instead, create your form on a separate web page (a landing page), and then add a hyperlink to that page within your email message.

887. Use a landing page for response

A landing page is the most popular way of responding to your offer. It works like this: your prospects click the link in your email message and are taken to your landing page. It will often include a form to fill out and submit to complete the transaction.

888. Don't send people from an email message to your homepage

If you're offering something to your email recipients in the email, send them via a hyperlink to a dedicated webpage (landing page) that is focused solely on the offer. That's because your homepage could prove to be too distracting for them so they forget the offer you've made, look around for a bit, and then leave.

889. Use a secure web page for transactions

Having a secure web page for your customer to complete a transaction will boost response to your email. Even if the transaction does not involve credit card payments, users prefer to fill out forms within a secure environment because they think their personal information will be in more trusted hands.

890. Restate the offer

Restate your offer on the landing page. You need to maintain momentum when your customer or prospect clicks through to the web form because, once they do, they rarely return to the originating email message.

891. Ask for what you need, and no more

Some marketers like to use landing pages as places to gather more data on their prospective customers – such as family income, occupation, etc. But the landing page is no place for market research. Even if you make it clear the information you are asking for is optional, your potential customer may still think you're invading their privacy and decide against the transaction. You can always find out that kind of information at a later time.

892. Adding to your in-house list

If you're using a rented list, the web form is a good place to ask your new customers if they would like to be added to your in-house list. If they agree, then you are free to email market to those customers for as long as they stay opted-in.

To apply for a free implementation session **worth £495** where we show you how everything in this book can be done for you, go to **completedigitalmarketingsystem.com/121**

245

893. Tell customers what happens next

If your customers place orders, let them know how long they'll have to wait for delivery. Send them an order number, a tracking number, and a telephone number to call in case there is a problem.

- If it's a subscription, let them know when they can expect the first issue

- If signing up for a seminar, send them a confirmation date

- If they are requesting information, tell them when they receive it

894. The final screen

When submitting a form, or sequence of forms, the final screen the users see should contain two messages: a confirmation that the order or request has been successfully received and a "thank you" for their business. If there is other information, such as tracking numbers and customer service, this is the place to include it.

895. Always include an opt out message

Email marketing is a permission-based medium. A surprising number of prospects will look for the opt-out instructions at the bottom of your email marketing message, even when they have no intention of opting out. This could be because having clear, opt-out instructions establishes some form of credibility.

896. Make it easy to opt out

Don't make people jump through virtual hoops to opt out of receiving your emails. Make it really simple and easy. Try something like this: "We respect your privacy, and promise not to abuse this method of contacting you. However, if you prefer not to receive further emails from us of this type, please click here and we will remove your contact information from our list."

897. Confirm opt-out status

Configure your opting-out procedures so that when users make this request, they receive a confirmation. This can take the form of a return email, or a web page telling the user that he or she is now off the list. A web page acknowledgement may be best because if you send people an email message after they've opted out, they're likely to assume you've just ignored their request.

898. Link to your privacy policy

Privacy is a big issue among web users. So, alleviate their concern with a link to your company's privacy policy. The best place for this within your email marketing message is below your opt-out instructions. But you can also add this link to your landing page as well.

899. Avoid words or phrases associated with spam or phishing messages

Email users are suspicious of messages that contain words or phrases associated with junk mail or phishing attempts. They also don't trust messages with subject lines that include strange or unfamiliar words. They're likely to regard the following words and phrases as suspicious:

- "Important information": although it seems like it might be a good way to attract users' attention, this term is too vague.

- "Confidential message": users don't like the suggestion that email contains confidential information. This term triggers fears of breached privacy and concerns about phishing.

Users may also be wary of the following words and terms:

- AgeingCredit report

- Degree

- Debt

- Advertise

- Diet

- Pain relief

- Prescription

- Salary

- Online

- Available

- Valued customer

900. Test more than the subject line of your emails

The subject line and content have historically been the elements people tested. But research by Marketing Sherpa found there are many other elements of your emails that are just as testable. They are:

- The subject line (phrasing, length, etc.)

- The message (the greeting, body, closing)

- Layout and images

- The call to action

- The days of the week sent

- Times of the day sent

- Personalisation

- Landing page

- Target audience

- From line

- Mobile layout and images

You could also test:

- Frequency
- Mostly images versus mostly text
- Links versus buttons
- The number of links
- Unsubscribe at the top
- First name personalisation in the subject line
- First name personalisation in the email body
- Animated gifs
- Font colours
- Font styles
- Social sharing icons
- Social connecting icons
- Call to action number
- Call to action placement
- Social proof
- Copy length
- Post-click landing page

Test one element at a time. If you try to test more than one at a time, you won't know which variant drove the success. Record your findings so you can refer back to check which variables you've tested. If possible, make testing your email marketing a daily occurrence, not something that you do once or twice a year.

901. Keep the same delivery time and day

If you're testing other variants than email timing (which time of the day and which day of the week is best), send your emails out at the same time and on the same day. That way, you'll eliminate the timing variant.

Chapter 10

Website Copy That Sells

In a Nutshell

Mere seconds is all you have to capture the interest of your website visitor. A video or amazing image will do some of the work in keeping your visitor's attention but most of it will come down to the text on your landing page.

Your copy is critical to your website's success. If it works, your visitor will stay to look around. If it fails, your visitor will leave and probably never return.

These tips will go a long way to making sure your website copy reaches out and grabs your visitor's attention.

902. Know your audience

Tailor your writing to suit the needs and interests of your target audience. Use words they use. Cover topics they're interested in.

903. Talk to your readers, not at them

Don't lecture your readers. Make the tone personal and use everyday language that people will understand immediately.

904. Use a conversational tone

Imagine you're sitting opposite a friend or colleague as you write. Don't patronise your readers.

905. Keep things active

Write in the active rather than the passive voice.

906. Spell out acronyms the first time you use them

While the majority of your readers will know what the UN stands for, many will have no clue about other acronyms. Get around this by spelling out the full name the first time you use it and putting the acronym in parenthesis next to it. For example, "Pay Per Click (PPC)". Thereafter, you can use the acronym.

907. Write succinctly

People are pressed for time and don't have the interest or patience to read ultra-long sentences that skirt around the point. Make your point and do it fast.

908. Use short sentences

Aim for 10-12 word sentences if your copy is aimed at consumers. If you're aiming at a corporate market, you can use slightly longer sentences (with say a maximum of 16 words).

909. Use one topic or idea per paragraph

Begin with a sentence about the topic of the paragraph and follow it with sentences that support that topic.

910. Use headings and subheadings to break up long sections of text and to make topics scannable

Make sure your headings are clear and easy to read. Write meaningful headings that match your readers' expectations. Avoid cute, clever, vague or alliterative headings that try to impress. You want them to act as signposts for the content.

911. Avoid using too many hyperlinks

Unless you're hyperlinking to a product or sales page, try to avoid using adding too many hyperlinks in your web page copy. Don't send visitors to other websites with your hyperlinks either. The point of the website is to get your prospective visitors to call you or buy from you or to request more information from you. If you send them off to other websites, your marketing efforts will only benefit the companies that own those sites.

912. Define the purpose of the page

This may sound obvious, but too few marketers establish a clear, clean purpose for a web page. Each web page should have one purpose.

All too often, web pages are treated like dumping grounds for content.

To avoid this on your website, decide what the purpose of each page is. What do you want the page to achieve?

- Close a sale?

- Secure a subscription or registration?

- Help people find a particular product or service page on your site?

- Invite participation?

- Pre-sell a product or service and then move the reader forward to a sales page?

- Educate the reader and then direct him or her forward to one of your main category pages?

Keep your answer in mind as you create the page. Don't deviate from that purpose.

913. Get clarity on your visitors' expectations

What do they want? What are they hoping for? What are their expectations?

There are clues and trails you can follow when trying to identify the specific purpose someone has in mind when coming to a page.

First, ask yourself where they came from. A link from the homepage? That link text will give you a very clear idea as to your page visitor's expectations. The same is true of someone arriving via a search engine. To find your page, they typed a few words into the search engine's search field. Those words give you a strong clue as to the visitor's expectations. If they came via a link in an email, what expectations did the email build up and set? What was the promise?

Follow these trails and do your best to determine the visitor's expectations.

You will always maximise the effectiveness of a web page by getting as close as you can to matching the visitor's expectations.

914. Match your reader's expectations immediately

Don't waste time or words. Get to the point fast. The web is not the place to write clever introductory text. It's not the place to do some grand scene-setting. Just get out of the way and let them do what they came there to do.

Whatever it is that they want, give it to them immediately.

915. Write only as much as you need to

A web page can have two lines of text or a thousand lines of text. There is no fixed length. The tendency online is to write more than is really necessary.

Don't do that.

Confirm what it is your visitor wants to do, and write only enough to enable them to meet their goal.

916. Tell people what to do

If your visitor takes no action after reading the web page, you have failed. You need them to do something. Hopefully, if you have done a good writing job, the link they click will correspond exactly to the expectations they had before they arrived at your site.

917. Write for visitors as well as search engines

Your web copy must make sense to your visitors.

918. Use bullet points to make your copy easier to scan and read

Bullet points make it easier for prospective customers to see the benefits your product or service delivers. That in turn makes it easier for them to 'digest' the benefits and think about them.

919. Get to the point fast on your website

Your website visitors will give your website about three seconds before deciding whether it is going to give them what they want. Your headline needs to grab their attention in those few seconds and encourage them to linger.

920. Get rid of the 'welcome' headline on your homepage

'Welcome' is the most predictable and boring of homepage headlines. It also says nothing of value or interest to your website visitors. Get rid of it and replace it with a headline that will capture the interest of your visitors and convey your website's value proposition.

921. Keep selling after the purchase is confirmed

The sales process is nowhere near complete when the customer presses the 'confirm purchase' button. He or she can cancel the order before it is shipped or downloaded, call your customer service department with queries or concerns regarding their order, or return the order after it has been delivered. To minimise the chances of any of these things happening, make sure your website features confirmation pages and that you send follow-up emails. They should all be written in a way that reassures your customer and helps them to feel good about their decision to buy your product or service.

922. Make your website headline work hard for you

The headline on your homepage or product/service page should:

- Say what it is

- Say what people get

- Say what people are able to do with it

Use your headline with a sub-headline to boost clarity. Follow this with a paragraph that explains the product or service then bullet points (about three) that emphasise the benefits.

923. Be specific and don't use hype

People are very sceptical about superlatives and hype online with good reason: there are far too many snake oil salesmen vying to offload some rubbish programme or product that has supposedly made them millions of pounds. That's why you must avoid using superlatives wherever possible. Provide specifics instead. For example, instead of saying, "The best life coach in Europe" say "Winner of Best Life Coach Award Three Years Running".

924. Provide proof for any claim you make

Always back up any claims you make about your product or service. If you don't, people will assume you're being "creative with the truth" (lying, in other words). How do you provide proof? Use testimonials (full first and last name and if possible a photograph or video), third party reviews, expert opinions or scientific studies.

925. Always put your customers first

Your copy should always be about your customers rather than your company. That's because your visitors' overriding interest is in themselves. They come to your website with a burning question, "What's in it for me?" They are not interested in you or your company (or your mission statement, values or vision, etc.). You need to convince them that your company has their best interests at heart. So use the word 'you' throughout your copy rather than 'we'.

926. Put your strongest benefits in your headlines or sub-headlines

Seconds is all you have to convince your website visitors that they've come to the right place. Since the first (and possibly only) place they'll look is the headline on the page, make sure your headline and sub-headline reveal the biggest benefits your product or service delivers. Don't save the 'best bits' to the main text – use them in your headline or sub-headline.

927. Tell people what they will lose if they don't get your product or service

Research has shown that people tend to respond more to a fear of loss than to a desire for gain (in other words, they're more worried about what they will lose than what they will get). So emphasise the loss aspect more than the gain aspect. Do of course test your target market to discover what motivates them.

928. Use trigger words in your calls to action

Avoid vague terms for your calls to action like 'Submit', 'Next' or 'Read more'. Instead use text that explains what the link or button offers. The exceptions to this are the expressions 'Click here' or 'Subscribe' – they work well. Your calls to action are among the many elements you should test so that you can determine what wording gets the best response from your target market.

929. Use quality product descriptions on ecommerce websites

Using quality product descriptions can boost conversion rates by 30% to 100%. Using unique copy for each product description rather than what was sent to you by the manufacturer can also increase search traffic dramatically. Don't, for example, use a product description that says, "XP-3RRD" because it will convey nothing of interest to your prospective customers. The only exception is if your customers all know what an XP-3RRD is and wouldn't know it by any other description.

930. Persuade and establish trust with your ecommerce copy

It's not easy, but your ecommerce must achieve two goals: establish trust with your visitor and persuade them that your product or service is perfect for them. Since they can't touch or see the product or service you're offering, your copy must anticipate their needs while at the same time convincing them your company is trustworthy.

931. Use a combination of bullets and paragraphs in ecommerce copy

Since most of your visitors will scan rather than read any web page, you need to use bullet points to communicate the key details and benefits of your product or service. Use paragraphs to add depth to your descriptions.

932. Avoid long sentences in ecommerce copy

Your sentences need to be easy to read and understand so keep them short. Long sentences are usually difficult to digest and therefore don't work as well as short sentences. Don't use too many adjectives and adverbs in your copy.

933. Don't use clichés or jargon

Keep in mind that the object is to sell your product or service and to do that, your prospects must be able to understand what you have written. Aim for clarity. Jargon can confuse or alienate visitors while clichés will probably bore them.

934. Keep things simple

You don't need to use your writing to convince people you're clever. Use your writing to convince them of the benefits of owning your product or using your service. That means your writing needs to be easy to understand. Avoid complex words in product descriptions.

935. Put some copy on all your product pages

Always include some copy on every product page on your website even if it has the most incredible product image or video. Copy is an important tool for persuasion and building trust so use it.

936. Don't exaggerate

You may want to describe your product or service as 'life changing' or 'revolutionary' but only do it if you've got statistics that prove that is the case. Don't exaggerate to make the product more desirable: this will cost your website authenticity and trust. Always use logically coherent arguments when explaining the benefits and applications of your product. It's alright to exaggerate the emotional response to a product, but not the product itself. Even if you increase sales through misrepresentation, the chargebacks, returns and negative reviews will eradicate any gains you might make.

937. Stick with what works

It can be tempting to get creative with the wording on buttons and links, but this is unlikely to be a good idea. Consumers have inbuilt notions of how to shop from their collective experience across thousands of websites. Stick with "Contact Us", "Add to basket" and factual, descriptive anchor text to link to product pages.

938. Establish trust

One of the most important things your website needs to do is establish trust. Customers are wary of spending money, particularly if they feel that they risk not receiving what they expect in return. The first way to establish trust is to have flawless copy. Grammar and spelling mistakes make you look careless and incompetent. If you can't put the time into flawless copy, visitors won't invest time and money into your products or services. Worse, they will doubt your professionalism.

939. State the obvious

Be clear when explaining payment, shipping, and returns processes – don't be afraid to state the obvious. If a customer is uncertain about any of these details they won't buy your products or use your services. It's that simple. Customers don't want to waste time on wondering whether payment and shipping will be carried out in accordance with their expectations. Keep things straight and clear: actual shipping costs and payment conditions shouldn't be displayed in tiny font sizes or be clarified using extra asterisks or footnotes.

One study showed that 20% of people have abandoned a purchase because shipping costs were unclear, so make sure your terms are easily understandable even when they aren't a selling point. Free shipping has such profoundly positive results that it's almost always worth apportioning the costs elsewhere and having minimum order requirements where necessary.

940. When appropriate, convey excitement in your copy

Use engaging phrases such as "Don't miss this!" and "Here's the best part..." but keep these to a minimum to avoid sounding too sales-y and distracting readers from your point.

941. Use contractions

Use contractions such as it's, don't, you'll, I'm, and we're. It will lend your copy a more conversational and relaxed feel.

942. Give your readers a "break"

Em dashes (–) and ellipses (...) help break up sentences into separate thoughts... and help your reader to digest ideas more easily. While they're not always acceptable within traditional publishing, you should feel free to use them when writing online. (If you're publishing your ezine in text format, use two hyphens to represent an em dash, like this: --.).

943. Use ALL CAPS rarely, if at all

While they make an impact when used occasionally, words in all caps are extremely hard to read. Caps also come across as "screaming" to your readers – not a good thing.

944. Go easy on the hype-y punctuation

Some people think that the more exclamation points you put after a sentence, the more effective it is. They're wrong. One does the job. The same applies with question marks – one is enough.

945. Use bullets and numbers to draw attention to lists and make them easier to read

Remember it's harder to read online than on paper, so keep your content organised for your readers. (If you're publishing in straight text, remember you can't use those automatic bullets that your word processing program creates. So just use hyphens (-), asterisks (*), or another keyboard symbol.)

946. Keep your paragraphs short and give them "white space"

Don't let any paragraph go on more than 10 lines or so. You can even make a single line its own paragraph to give it emphasis. And put at least one line in between each paragraph.

947. Break up long articles with subheads

Like mini-headlines, subheads are effective in bringing out key points for your readers. And they also help make any long article easier to read because they break up long blocks of text into easy-to-digest bits.

948. Limit your descriptive words

Instead of using three or four adjectives to describe a feature of your product, come up with one powerfully descriptive word.

949. Print before you send or publish

Mistakes are easy to miss when reading online – even professional proof-readers insist on printing all pages of a website for reviewing. You'll be amazed at how many more mistakes you'll catch on paper.

950. Grab readers' attention with great headlines

You should spend almost as much time developing your headlines as you do your body copy.

Why?

The first thing a reader sees on his screen can mean the difference between your success and failure. If your first impression is boring or irrelevant, your prospects will not read on. Your headlines need to both get attention and convey what's coming up – quickly. Make your headline appeal to your reader's interests and concerns – not yours. Remember, it's not about you.

A strong headline can:

- Highlight a benefit

- Summarise content

- Spark reader interest

951. Ask a question in your headline

This type of headline automatically gets your readers involved in your message because they answer the question in their minds. Many people will read further just to find out what answer or solution you provide.

952. Tell them "how to"

People love information that shows them how to do something. Think of the benefits your service/product offers and then try creating some "how to" headlines.

953. Give a command in your headline

Turn your most important benefit into a commanding headline – you're essentially telling the reader what to do.

954. Use a number in the headline

Readers love numbers so use them in your headline (for example, "Seven reasons why…"). Numbers easily "package" the idea you're selling.

955. Use specific numbers in your copy

When it comes to numbers, specific beats general. Specific numbers make the statement more believable and will bring better results. It's crucial that your service is "easy" to use and get the desired results. People buy simplicity, not complications.

956. Use power words in your headlines

Here are some power words that will make your headline irresistible:

- How/how to
- You
- Free
- Discover
- Guaranteed
- New
- Announcing
- Now
- Easy
- Health
- Love
- Proven
- Save
- Safety
- Attention:

Incorporate these words into your headline, where appropriate, and watch your response rates soar.

957. Avoid making mistakes with your headlines

If you want your headlines to sell:

- Don't be a comedian
Don't use headlines that try to be clever, cute, or use a play on words. This is definitely NOT the way to get attention and entice readers to take action.

- DON'T USE ALL CAPITAL LETTERS
Capitals will not make your headline more effective. People are just not accustomed to reading words in all capital letters. This just makes it more difficult on the eyes and harder to read. Occasional words may be capitalised for emphasis, but not your entire headline.

- Don't use excessive punctuation!!!!!!!! Besides looking amateurish, it screams "hype" from a mile away.

- Don't Let Graphics (or Anything Else) Take Attention Away from Your Headline. The headline is the most important part of your sales piece. Any distractions will hinder results. You can use graphics to enhance your sales piece, but not to distract from its purpose

- Don't try to get everyone's attention with your headline

If you have the mind-set that your service or product is for everyone, you've already lost. Only a specific group of people will respond to your offer. And you should only attempt to reach that specific audience with your headline (and all your other marketing materials).

958. Try positive or negative headlines

A headline should include a benefit that will appeal to your readers, whether that benefit is a positive or a negative. Positive headlines can insinuate:

- Saving

- Profiting

- Gaining

- Winning

- Rewarding

Positive headlines focus in on the rewards that your readership will gain if they continue to read your copy. Examples:

- "Reward yourself with a 20% saving"

- "Gain an edge over the competition"

Negative headlines allude to:

- Loss

- Embarrassment

- Mistakes

- Uneasiness

- Pain

Negative headlines can be written to help readers avoid making any unnecessary blunders that will make their lives miserable. Examples:

- "Do you have lousy clients that won't pay what they owe?"

- "Have you even been embarrassed at an expensive restaurant?"

- "Avoid the pain of bankruptcy"

- "Do you ache at the end of the day?"

959. Use appealing headlines

Everyone loves to be part of the 'in-crowd'. Headlines that can hook with the in-crowd in mind include words such as 'secret' or 'little known ways'.

Some examples are:

- "The secrets of beauty supply management"
- "Little known ways to improve your bottom line"

On the flip side of the coin, no one wants to be left out. "What everyone should know about growing roses" screams at the reader that he or she may not have the complete story and really needs to check the content out to make sure that the reader 'knows it all'.

960. Appeal to time-poor readers with easy and time-saving headlines

Most people hate wasting time, particularly on solving problems. Many would like to ignore their problems. They hope that the problems would just go away. Consequently, headlines that emphasise speed in solving a problem can be real winners. Examples include:

- "Five quick ways to fix a drain"
- "A quick way to house-train your dog"

No one likes to do things that are difficult. Therefore, 'easy' is another great hook word. Examples of headlines:

- "Five easy ways to study more effectively"
- "One easy way to pick up incremental sales"

'Easy' can also be combined with 'quick' for a 'double whammy' headline. Example:

- "Five quick and easy steps to program your DVD player"

If your target markets includes people who are challenged by issues such as technology or home repairs, 'easy' is a nice word to have in your arsenal.

A variation of 'easy' is the 'lazy' approach:

- "A lazy person's way of doing laundry"

Lazy implies that the content will give information about how to do laundry quickly and easily.

961. Curiosity-inducing headlines are hard to ignore

Curiosity is a strong motivation to learn more. A headline that appeals to curiosity would be:

- "Ways to entice your wife or girlfriend"
- "Interested in getting the goods?"
- "The alluring world of insects"

962. 'Just the facts' headlines may be all you need

Sometimes simply stating the facts is a good way to go with headlines.

- "Learn how mid-size companies use LinkedIn to manage their business"

- "Ten time management techniques"

963. Strive to understand what's going on in the reader's mind

Attempt to allay any fears or doubts your readers may have. When you do this, the reader will have the perception that you understand and care about him or her and in turn will begin to care about and understand you – thus greatly increasing your chances for making the sale.

964. Offer B2B prospects a white paper

A white paper is usually five to 10 pages in length and describes a new technology, methodology, or best practice. B2B companies use white papers to generate sales leads, get publicity and position themselves as thought-leaders in an industry.

965. Write to sell, not to impress

Put the thesaurus away. The point of your copy is to increase sales and profits, not to make people gasp in astonishment at your cleverness.

966. Sell one thing at a time

Focus on selling just one service or one idea. You can always tell clients about all your other fabulous services or products later.

967. Don't cram your copy with keywords

In Search Engine Optimization 'speak', this is called "keyphrase stuffing" or "keyword stuffing" – and could actually get your website penalised by the search engines. According to Google's Webmaster guidelines: "Filling pages with keywords results in a negative user experience, and can harm your site's ranking. Focus on creating useful, information-rich content that uses keywords appropriately and in context."

968. Limit the number of keywords on any web page

Don't use more than five keywords on any one web page.

969. Be specific in your copy

Being specific makes your copy more believable. The more details you can share, the more likely your prospect will be convinced that you are telling the truth.

970. Avoid limp words in your copy

Steer clear of words that are too limp, too vague, to carry any impact.

They're words like:

- It – tell people what 'it' is rather than leaving them to work out what you're on about

- Quality – every product or service has some quality – good or bad

- Tastiest

- Best

- Fastest

- Strongest

- Superior

- Minimise

- Optimise

- Solution

- Technology

- Difference

Saying your product or service is 'superior' or the 'strongest' will create doubt in your prospects' minds. Superlatives on their own appear unsubstantiated. They lack power because they are not measurable.

Be specific. The more specific your message, the more believable you will appear.

971. Practise writing

The only way you can get better at writing is to write continually, even when you don't feel like writing. This doesn't mean that you have to keep writing all day but you should write often enough so that you develop the discipline to write even when you don't feel like writing.

972. Use stories in sales letters

An effective and compelling story is one of the most powerful devices in sales letter writing. People are always interested in stories about other people.

973. If you offer a list in a sales letter make each point progressively shorter

World-class copywriter Clayton Makepeace says if you offer a list ("Seven Ways To...") in a sales letter, make each one progressively shorter (the first point might be a page and a half long, the next might be half a page and the sixth and seventh points might just be bullet points). This will create a sense of momentum for the reader that lets them feel as if they're zipping through the copy while deriving great benefit.

974. Overcome objections with a story

A story can override your prospects' initial objections and resistance. A story creates empathy with the reader and helps to draw him into the sales pitch. This works best if the story identifies with the problem that the prospect is now experiencing for which you've found the solution.

975. Build up the value of your product just before you present the price

You can do this by summarising your strongest benefits and compare the price your prospects pay to what it will cost them to create the product for themselves. Let them 'feel' the deal they are getting.

976. Use sentences of different lengths to vary the cadence and rhythm of the paragraph

All sentences of the same length will make the copy seem mechanical and dry.

977. Appeal to your readers' emotions and not just logic

Most people make a decision based on emotion and then try to justify the decision with logic. Fill your copy with emotive words.

978. Trim the fat

Most sentences are flabby: filled with puffery and excessive verbiage. To make your sentences lean and powerful, use as few words as possible to get your idea across. Prune your sentences to their essential components and don't waste one word.

979. Good writing is concise

This does not mean that every sentence should be short, or omit details about your subject, but every word should count. For example, instead of using the phrase "owing to the fact that", use "since"; replace "at this point in time" with "now"; and so on.

980. Read your copy aloud

Once you've finished writing your web page, blog post, email, or sales letter, read it aloud. You'll become aware of faulty sentence structures, mistyped words, or repetitions as you do.

981. Write case studies to capture prospects' interests

Case studies work like testimonials on steroids because they demonstrate specific examples of how your product or service solved the type of problem or challenge your prospect has.

982. Your case study should be short, candid and revealing

The best case studies are ones that sound like a legitimate problem. The reader wants candour. They want to see the pain point. They want something to be revealed.

The case study has to be specific and easily digestible. It has to be tactical information that can be generalised. Unless you have results, the case study is not nearly as powerful as it should be.

983. Stick to a word count with your case study

Keep to a limit of around 500 words for your case study. If your readers can't skim quickly to get the gist, you're wasting your efforts.

984. Make your case study specific

The more specific you are, the greater the impact of your case study.

985. Structure your case study

There are three sections to a case study:

1. Problem
2. Implementation
3. Results

Your case study should follow that structure.

986. The opening 'problem' section in your case study must carry a punch.

Your opening problem has to mean something to the reader – something that they can relate to. Always write about an issue that has significant business impact for the reader. Demonstrate how your product resolved a critical business issue – what you're implying in this section is that if they choose your product or service, you can also resolve their issues. Indeed, the more specific the case study, the more effective it will be. Case studies that propose to 'solve all problems' are not taken seriously.

987. Don't dilute the case study by addressing more the one issue

Stick to one area and explain how you solved a problem in measurable and quantifiable terms. For example:

- Support your case study with statistics, figures, and tables where appropriate.

- Return on investment – explain how the investment in your product/service pays for itself. For example, it increases productivity by 50% within two months. Demonstrate how you can substantiate this; otherwise, your argument loses credibility.

- Cost containment – how does the solution help contain costs? This area is very important, as budgets are always a sensitive issue. If you can illustrate how a similar company saved a certain amount of money by adopting your product – i.e. real proof – you'll certainly capture the reader's attention.

- Reducing barriers – demonstrate how your solution improves operations. For example, how does it fit into their business process? This is a good area to mention how your system plugs into other applications or expensive, business critical equipment.

 To apply for a free implementation session **worth £495** where we show you how everything in this book can be done for you, go to **completedigitalmarketingsystem.com/121**

988. Write effective case studies

A well-written case study should:

- build suspense
- have a satisfying conclusion
- solve a generalisable business problem (make money or save money)

If the objective is to showcase your organisation's capabilities, it may also propel the reader into the first step of the buying process for your product or service.

- Start with a compelling, results-driven headline. Include a benefit in the title of your case study.

- Your first paragraph should focus on a summary of the case, focusing on a one-sentence description of the problem, and then how you solved the problem.

- Define the problem in more detail.

- Define your solution. Avoid technical jargon.

- Define the results. Here it is best to have the client provide a quote testifying to the results. That increases your credibility 100%.

- Have a side bar that summarises the case (the way magazines have boxes with large text and summaries for readers who just want to skim).

- Provide facts and figures–especially about saving or making more money.

- Speak in your customers' language, not yours.

- Break up your text with compelling subheadings.

989. Use proof in your case study

Support your claim with statistics and testimonials. You need to show how the investment in your product/service is worthwhile (provide tangible results). Without some kind of proof, your case study loses credibility.

990. Don't make your case study too technical

Your case study needs to be interesting and easy to read so go easy with technical terms or descriptions. Similarly, don't go crazy with graphs and tables.

991. Interview your client for your case study

Interview your client for your case study. Ask your client to tell you:

- What solution they were looking for when they hired you?

- What did you provide that they valued the most?

- What is the result of working with you?

- What would they tell others who are considering hiring you?

Get their replies transcribed. Use the transcription as the basis of your case study. Use the language your client used because it's most likely the same way your prospects talk.

992. Write compelling articles

Writing articles is a great way to drive traffic to your website, get established as an expert in your field, and get your name out to thousands of people which will establish your credibility.

993. Use the resource box at the end of articles to get more clients

Resource boxes are usually where writers tell readers a little about themselves. Forget that! Use it to get readers to your website or special landing page. How? Offer them something they won't be able to resist, like a special report on the same subject. Add a hyperlink that takes them to the landing page.

994. Don't write your article like a sales letter

The purpose of your article is to get leads for your business but that doesn't mean you should write it like a sales letter. It needs to provide something interesting, relevant, or useful to your prospect.

995. Convey your website's value proposition

The value proposition is generally the first sentence that your visitor will scan on your site. With that one sentence, you should convey the credibility of your company and quantify exactly what sets you apart from all other companies online. It should tell your ideal customer why they should use your services and not those of your top competitors.

The value proposition is usually a block of text (a headline, sub-headline, and one paragraph of text) with a visual (photo, hero shot, graphics).

- The headline must grab your prospects' attention and it should encapsulate the end-benefit you're offering in one brief sentence. You can mention the product/service and/or the customer.

- A sub-headline or a two to three sentence paragraph should provide a specific explanation of what you do/offer, for whom and why it is useful.

- Use three bullet points to list the key benefits of your products and services.

Why use a value proposition? Companies who test their value propositions are 15% more likely to produce a return on investment for their websites. That's a 15% bump in performance by changing a single sentence, which is a pretty compelling argument for doing it.

996. Never assume people will understand what you're offering

Web usability guru Jakob Nielsen says you should never assume that people will know who you are and what you do when they arrive at your website. "Always provide a straightforward description of your company's purpose throughout your site," he says.

997. Your lead sentence must engage people so they continue reading

While your headline is an important tool in getting visitors to stay on your page, an engaging lead or first sentence will get visitors to read more.

There are a number of standard types of leads that can help get your copy read and a few are listed below:

- The question lead

The question lead can be used to create a sense of need in the reader – "Leaky washing machine?" The question lead makes the reader want to continue in search of a solution to the problem highlighted by the question.

- The teaser lead

The teaser lead can create intrigue about the information to follow. Example: "You're probably wealthier than you think."

- The summary lead

In cases of long copy, a summary lead can be used to set up the information to follow in a way that will make it easier to digest. Using a summary lead will allow you to get more of your important information out early, in the first sentence and above the fold (the part of the landing page that is visible on a PC).

Example: "With over 10,000 subscribers, the 'XYZ' newsletter is the most read industry resource available online."

- The direct address lead

Readers are more likely to relate your message to their needs if you specifically identify them in your copy. Even if they clicked the link to your landing page, they do not necessarily want to know about your company or what it can do for them. All they want to know is that you understand their problem or needs and can provide a solution.

Example: "You deserve a holiday today."

Again, you don't have a lot of time to get your visitors hooked and an engaging lead sentence will make the job easier. Maintain continuity and congruency by keeping your headlines, leads and link copy consistent to avoid confusing your visitor.

998. Your landing page copy needs to be persuasive and compelling

You can't just use any old words and plonk them on to your landing page. They simply won't do the job. What you need is copy that is crafted in a way that is proven to capture the attention of people online.

It has to do more than grab their attention however. It must also hold their interest and then convince them to take action – to respond to what they read. And that is why you must use the AIDA Formula.

The AIDA Formula is something that every great copywriter uses to craft copy that sells products and services in any business.

AIDA is an acronym for the key actions you need your prospective customers to take: that's Attention, Interest, Desire, and Action. The copy must always grab attention, hold interest, increase desire, and inspire action. It always has to be done in that order.

To get people's attention, headlines are crucially important. Headings can be:

- Question-based. The headline asks people something you know they want the answer/solution to.

- Problem-based. The headline is about a critical business problem your services can solve.

- How to. The headline tells people something you know they want to do.

- Curiosity factor. The headline stirs people's curiosity in a way that compels them to read on.

- Testimonials. The headline features other people telling your prospective clients how amazing your company's services are.

To really grab your reader's attention, you need to put the **benefits** rather than the **features** of your service in the headline.

To capture readers' **interest**, use details in the content that they will be able to relate to. Those details can include facts, stories, anecdotes, etc. The copy needs to answer every reader's unspoken question: What's in it for me? The copy must interest and relate to your reader, not your company.

To create **desire** for your service in your readers, use power words that trigger excitement and convey a mood.

You then need to tell your reader to take **action** so they can receive the benefits you've highlighted. Let them know the benefits of taking action and the pain they'll experience if they don't take action.

It's important to tell them exactly what action they need to take.

999. Use a call to action at the end of your video

A strong call to action is what separates an expensive but money-losing video from a profitable one with a strong return on investment. A call to action can be a command, a declarative statement or even just a suggestion.

Your call to action should be clear, concise and compelling. A compelling statement drives viewers to take action. And as for being clear and concise, the more quickly and easily the action can be completed, the greater your conversion rate will be.

Because the call to action is so important, ideally it should remain on screen for the entire duration of your message. If that's not practical, consider showing it several times during the video.

Start the call to action with a verb and keep the verb and subject close together.

Since actions that can be taken immediately tend to convert best, focus on those – just make sure you don't tell a viewer to do something that they can't or likely won't do.

Use trigger words to grab your viewer's attention. Words like Money, Discovery, Save, Easy, New, Proven, You, Results, Guaranteed and Safety can make otherwise uncommitted viewers snap to attention.

Use action words and be vivid. Use action words that help paint vivid pictures in the mind.

Use commands. Tell your audience exactly what you want them to do, and provided it's easy enough (or has a big enough potential upside for them), they might just do it.

1000. Create an About Us page people will want to read

Your About page is one of the most important pages on your site. Done right, it can help boost rankings and stimulate inbound links.

Most of your site's readers will visit your About Us page if they can find it. Missing About pages are a major reason for visitors' choosing to leave sites without conducting business.

This all makes sense: you can't expect people to do business with you without getting to know you first–and many of them don't know about you when they land on your site.

Present your information at four levels of detail:

- **A descriptive tagline.** On the homepage, briefly summarise what your organisation does.

- **More detail.** At the top of the 'About Us' page, offer one to two paragraphs about the benefits the organisation provides to customers in its products or services.

- **A fact sheet.** Following the summary, develop a section that elaborates on key points and other essential facts about the organisation.

- **Additional information.** Add subsidiary pages providing more in-depth or specialised information about the organisation.

To develop useful content, formulate a list of questions a potential customer might have about you, and address them. A starting point? Answer the journalist's 5 W's: who, what, where, when and why.

Take the time to be transparent. The more information you provide a prospective customer about yourself and your business, the better.

1001. Do a search of your website for the word 'we'

Your website copy should be entirely focused on your prospects. That means your copy should be about them not you or your company. You might think you've created a completely customer-centric website but it's highly likely that there are places where the word 'we' outnumbers the word 'you'. Do a check – search your website for 'we', 'I', and 'us'. If possible, replace those words with 'you' and 'your'.

How NABO Will Help You Get High Quality Leads

Now that you're armed with more than a thousand ways to get customers, there is only one key obstacle that stands between you and the financial freedom that you've worked so hard to achieve. That obstacle can be summed up in one word:

IMPLEMENTATION – in other words, 'getting things done'.

You're a smart business owner or you wouldn't even be reading this. You realise that everything boils down to getting CUSTOMERS. You now know that to achieve that, you need to sort out and improve your marketing. You know that you need to sort out your website and internet strategy. You know that you should be doing online video, producing a lead generating 'top tips' report for potential customers, maximising Google AdWords, creating a professional social media presence, sending regular customer emails – the list can sometimes seem endless.

But you know all that. The problem has been, who is going to do all of it? Who will do it properly and who can you trust to make your marketing happen for you quickly and professionally?

The problem is always – IMPLEMENTATION...

Now, we have the solution: your 'Complete Digital Marketing System.'

This system incorporates the TEN essential elements that MUST be part of your marketing and internet strategy – if your business is to attract the customers you need to survive and thrive in the years ahead.

AT A GLANCE

The Complete Digital Marketing System...

1. GREAT ONLINE VIDEO TO GENERATE MORE CONVERSIONS

Six videos to use on your site to turn visitors into sales – professionally filmed and edited in HD.

2. YOUR NEW LEAD GENERATION MICROSITE

A new microsite to convert your AdWords traffic into brand new business enquiries – consisting of a high performing landing page and video content – all written and designed for you.

3. EASY EMAIL MARKETING SET UP FOR YOU

We'll set up an email marketing system for you to use – we'll link it to the data capture form we'll give you for your main website and also to your new microsite. From day one you'll be building a list of people who are all future customers. We'll turn those anonymous website visitors into 'real people' – names and emails of people who are seriously interested in what you do, giving you new sales leads every day.

4. 52 WEEK EMAIL MARKETING CONTENT

We'll create for you a year of email marketing content, all set up in an autoresponder sequence so they go out every week without you having to worry about sending them. Each email will have a strong call to action and be designed to build sales for your company.

5. NEW WEBSITE HOME PAGE COPY

Our top copywriting team will transform your homepage by rewriting the copy on the page. These are the most important words in your business and will work hard to transform visitors into prospects and buyers.

6. YOUR OWN LEAD GENERATING 'TOP TIPS' REPORT

We'll interview you, write, edit and proofread a 'top tips' report. When you've approved it, we'll design it and create the PDF that is automatically sent to anyone who signs up on your microsite and website.

7. 52 WEEK FACEBOOK LEAD GENERATION UPDATES

We will create for you a professionally produced Facebook business page to instantly connect you to tens of thousands of potential customers on Facebook. Then we'll create 52 posts to promote your business every week of the year, automatically posted so you don't have to do anything.

8. INSTANT GOOGLE TRAFFIC

We'll create and write a Google AdWords campaign to send sales leads to your microsite which in turn will transform the most interested visitors into new sales leads that will then receive your PDF report and the email follow up sequence. You could be receiving new sales leads within thirty minutes of switching it on...

9. THE POWER OF RE-MARKETING

Tap into the latest and most powerful breakthrough in online marketing. When people visit your competitor's website and don't buy, your competitor has lost them forever. However, you'll be able to advertise to all of your website visitors for up to 18 months after they have been to your site, using Re-Marketing. We'll create a Re-Marketing campaign for you and create six powerful banner ads to win customers and boost sales.

10. ONGOING ONLINE SUPPORT, ADVICE AND STRATEGY

We all need some inspiration from time to time – and this online resource centre is a growing library of 'how to' videos, answering the questions our customers ask us – including yours. Want to know how to do something? We'll share the answer by video for other business owners to benefit from too. You need never be stuck not knowing what to do ever again.

If you're ready to take the next step now and see just how quickly you can transform your website, your online marketing and your profits then <u>apply</u> for your FREE face to face online strategy session worth £495. Simply head to:

completedigitalmarketingsystem.com/121

Notes

Notes

To apply for a free implementation session **worth £495** where we show you how everything
in this book can be done for you, go to **completedigitalmarketingsystem.com/121**

Notes

Notes

To apply for a free implementation session **worth £495** where we show you how everything
in this book can be done for you, go to **completedigitalmarketingsystem.com/121**